I0484340

Original Photographs 2014

Decades of being around accomplished talent producing absolutely phenomenal quality work has taught that we are capable of greatness. It is possible to meet our destiny and become it. Experiencing excellence done with such apparent ease and humble selfless gratification is the motivation for this photography. Most important was having the freedom

Being colorblind gives an advantage when composing black & white… less confusion. This special collection selected from thousands of captures. All images were framed in the camera and presented without edits, genuine as seen through the lens. RAW conversion applied by proprietary panchromatic process.

Limited edition fine art available from source files.

info@ BEACHNOISE.com

Joseph Fleming

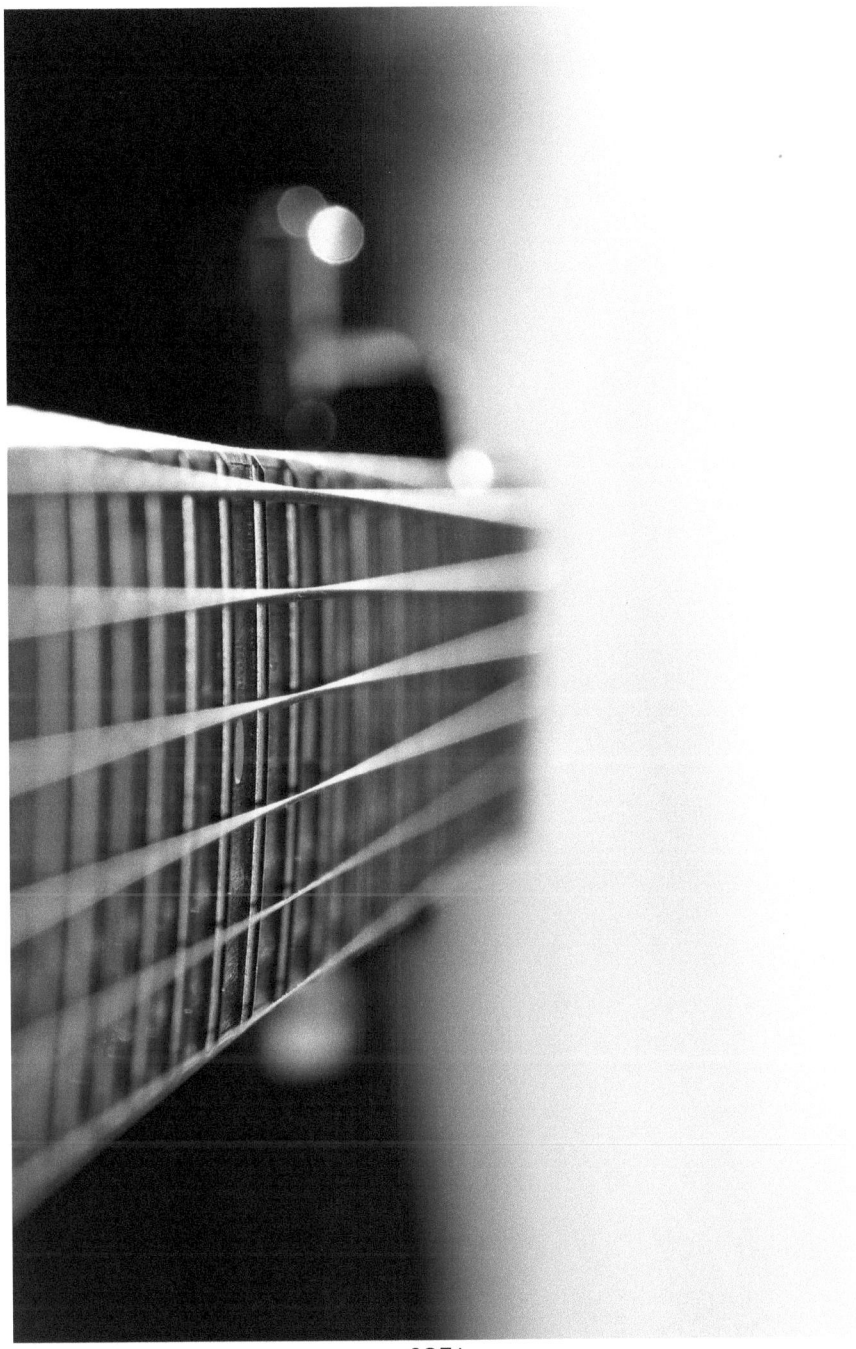

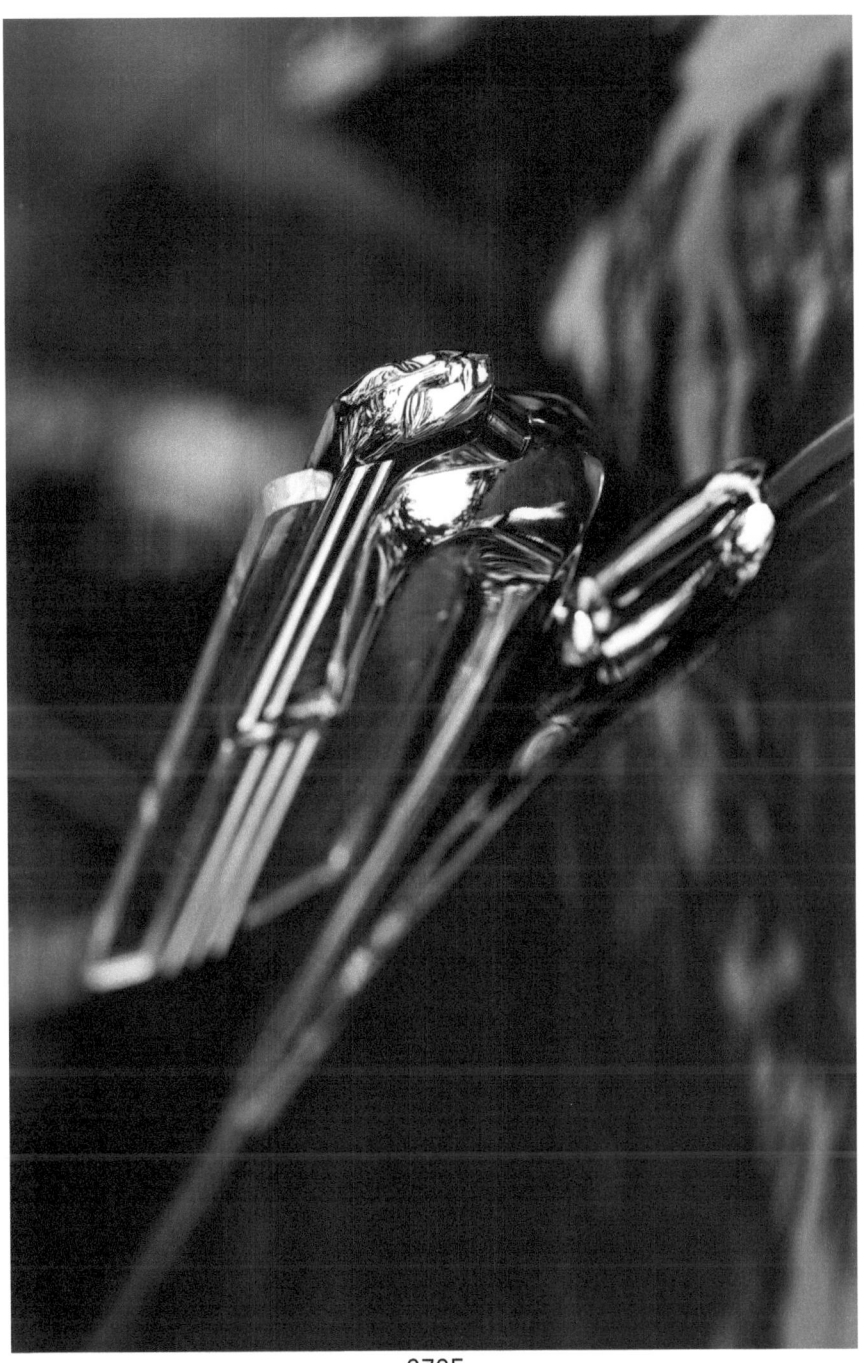

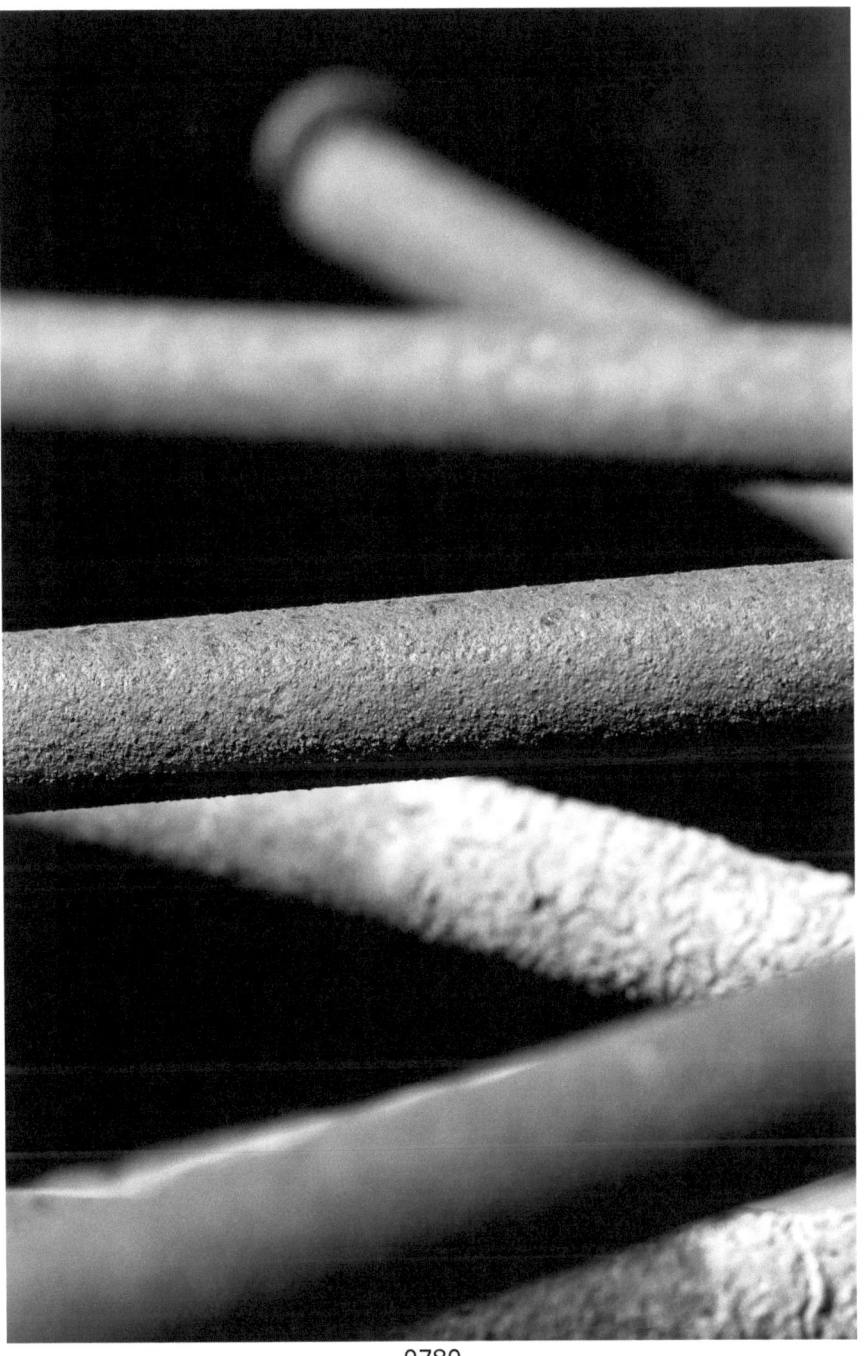

0780

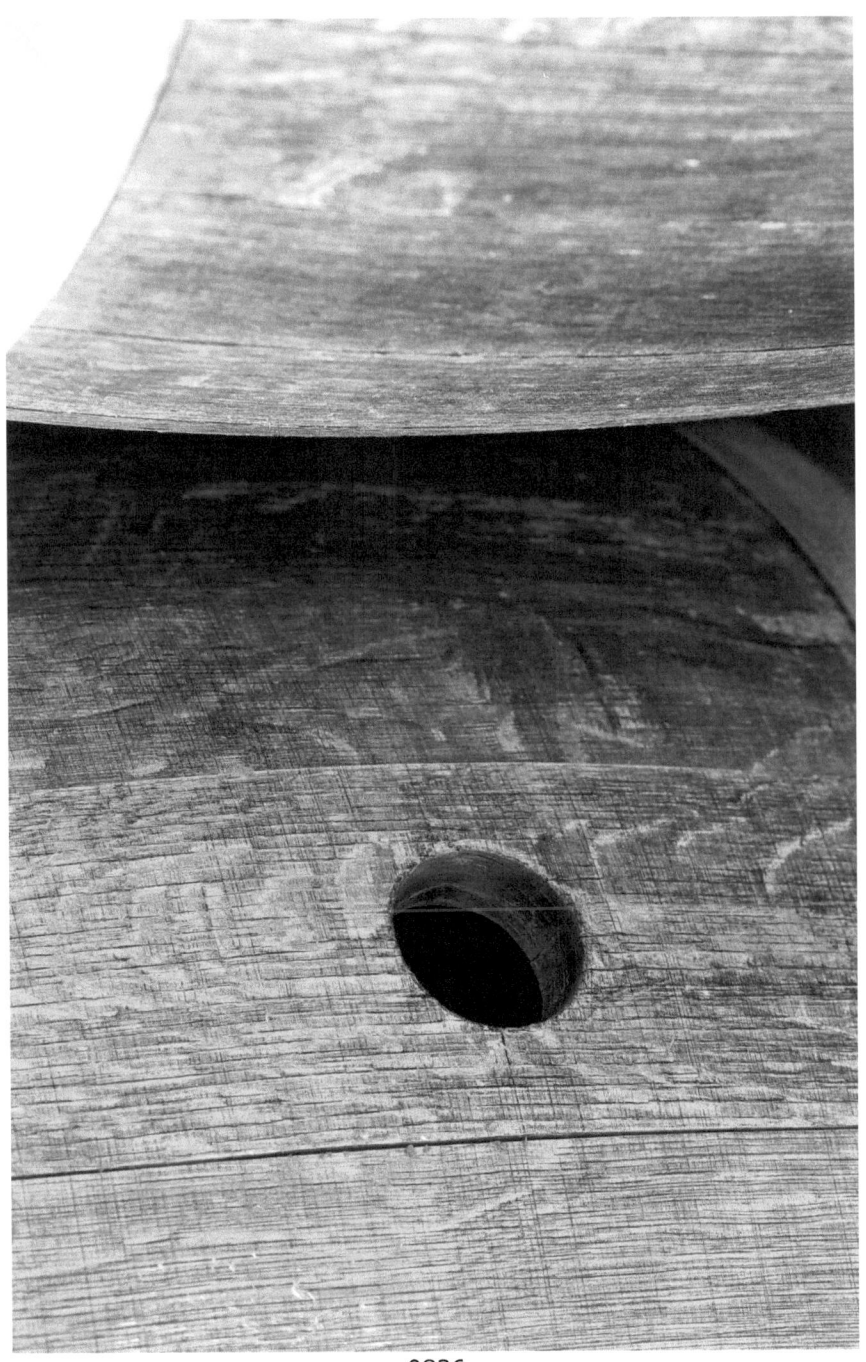

0826

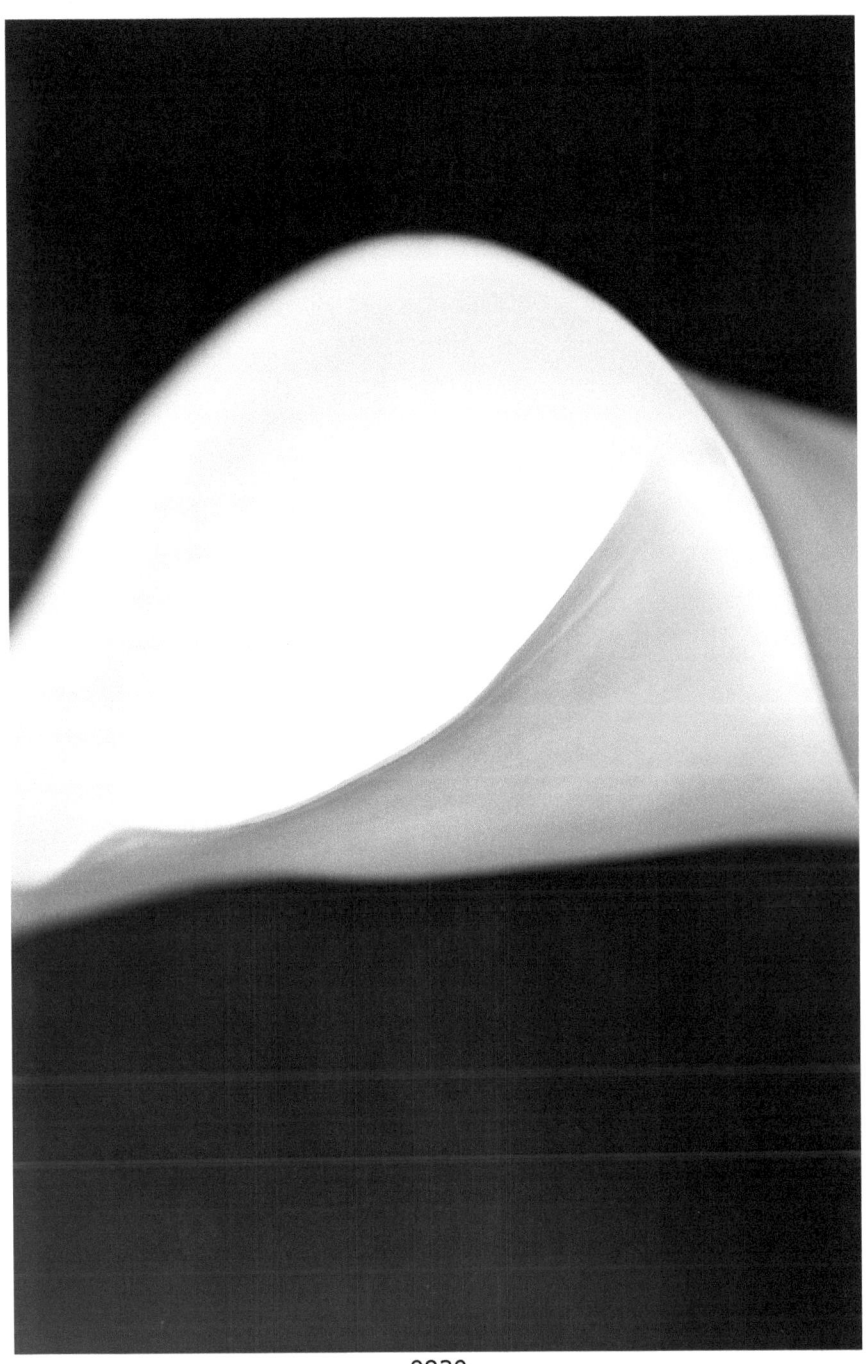

0920

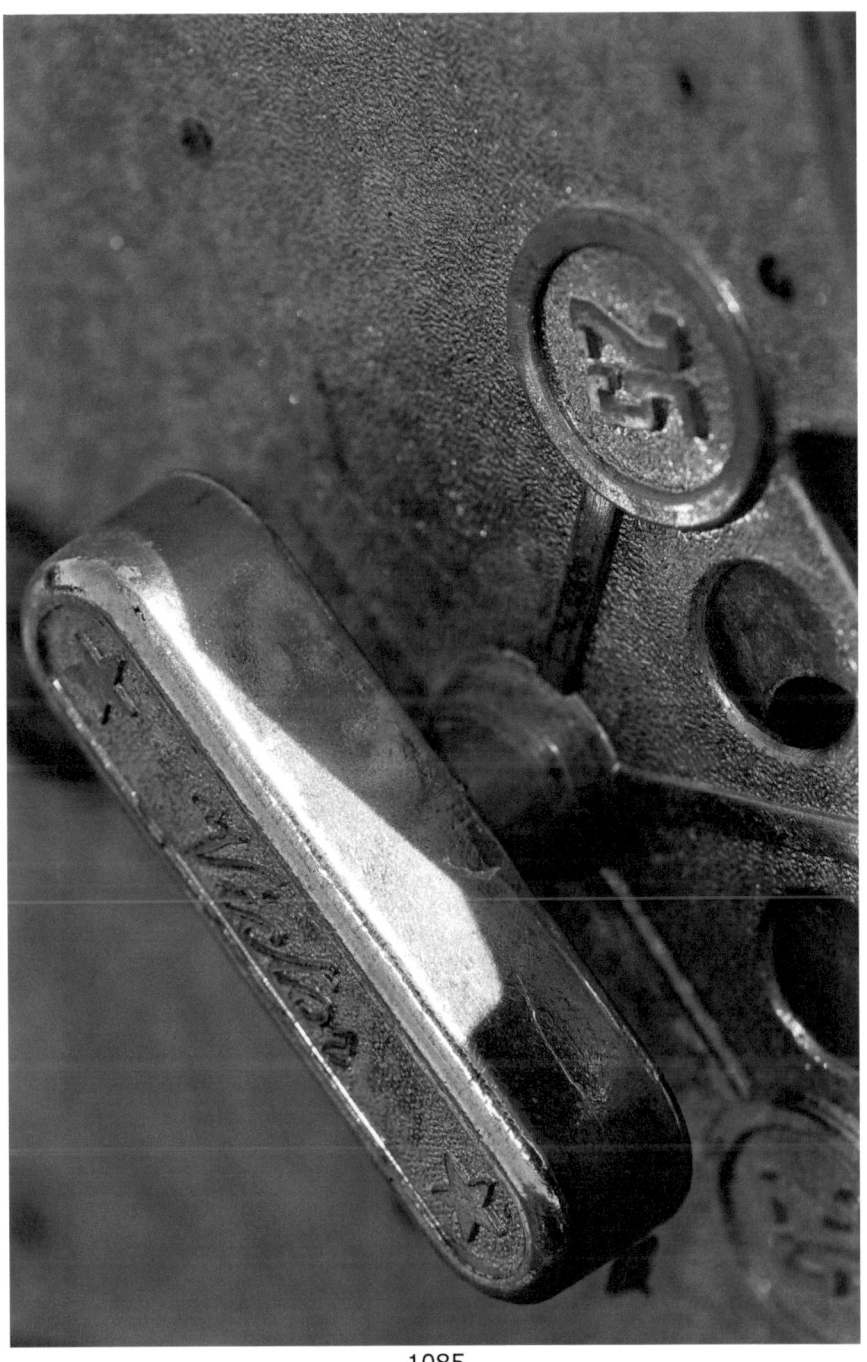

1085

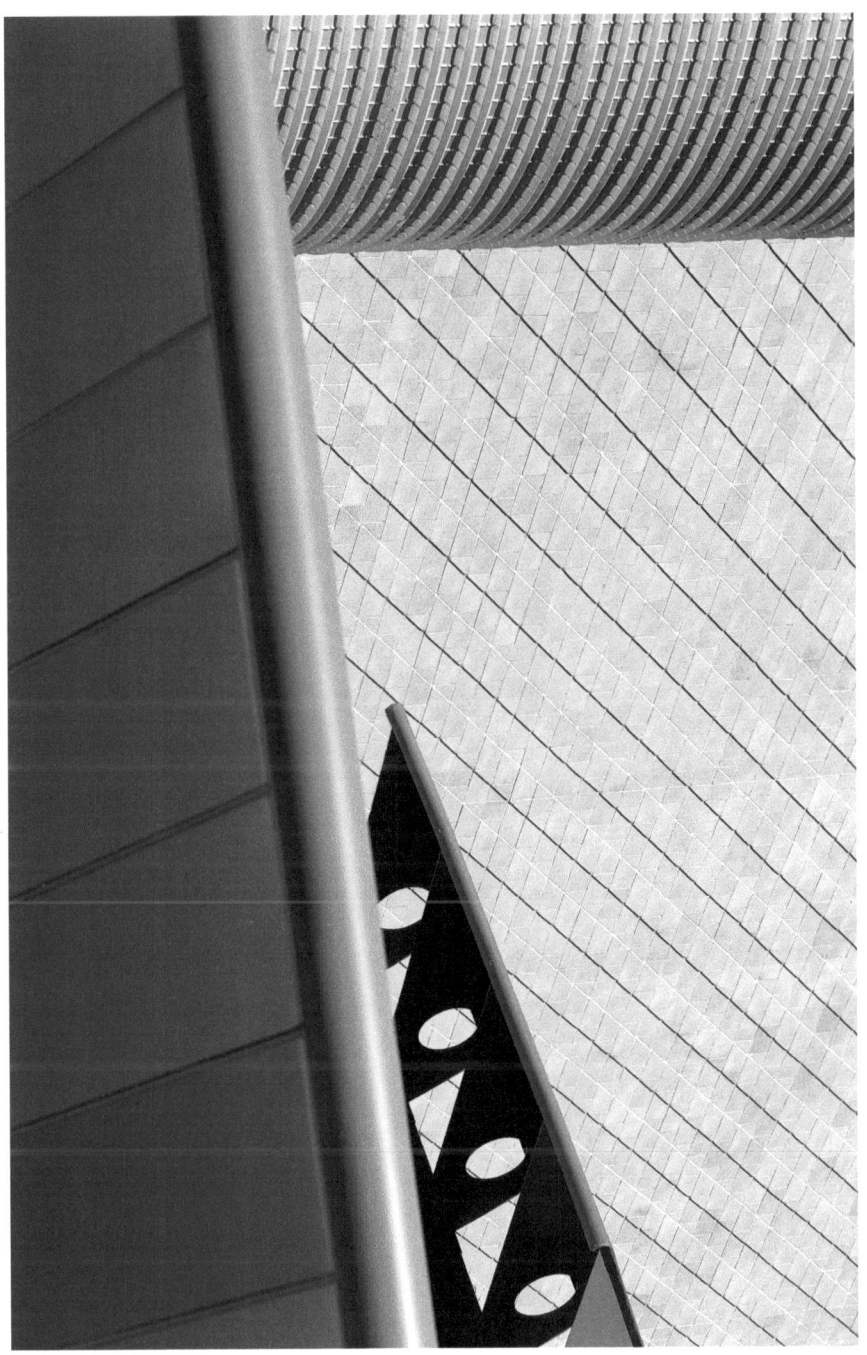

1088

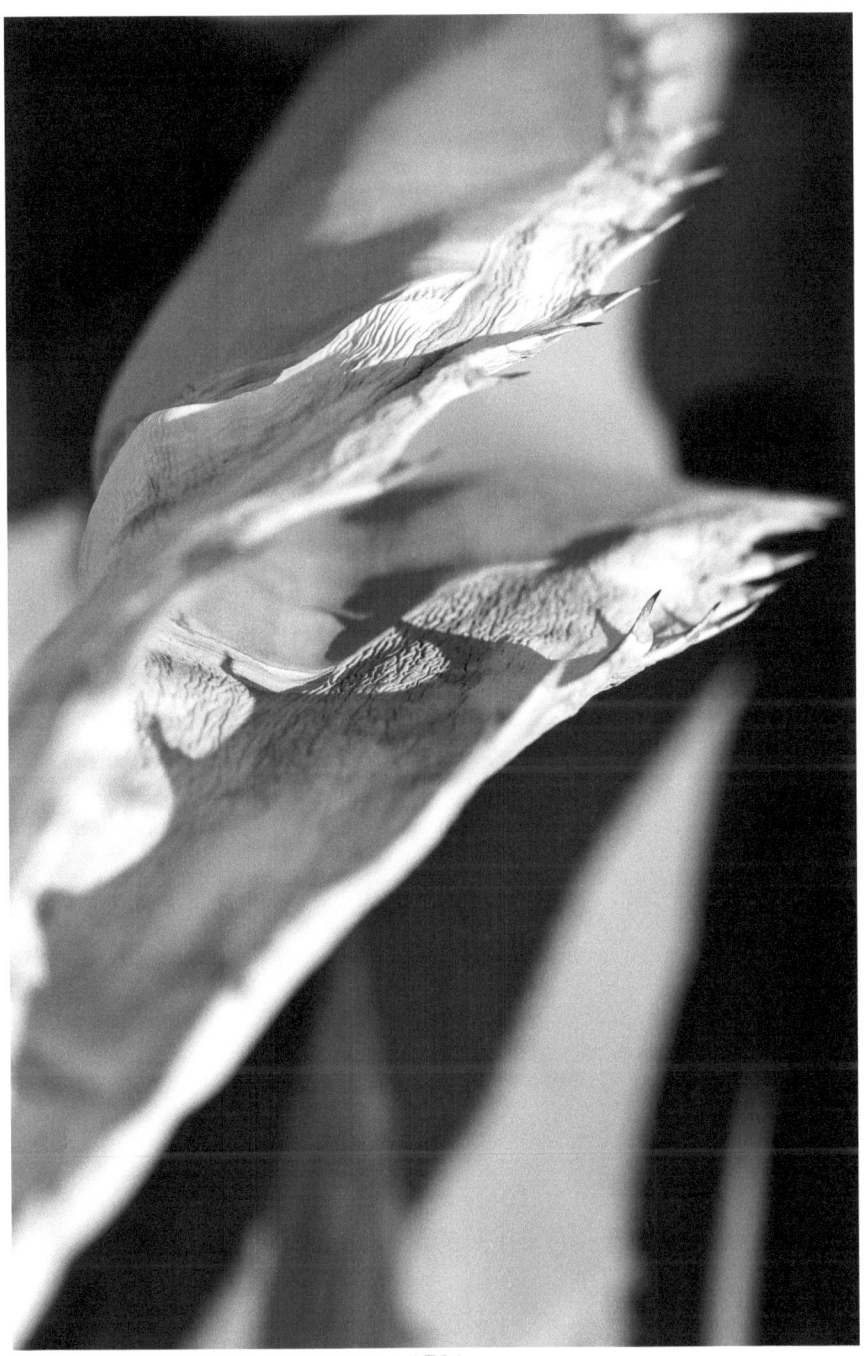

1581

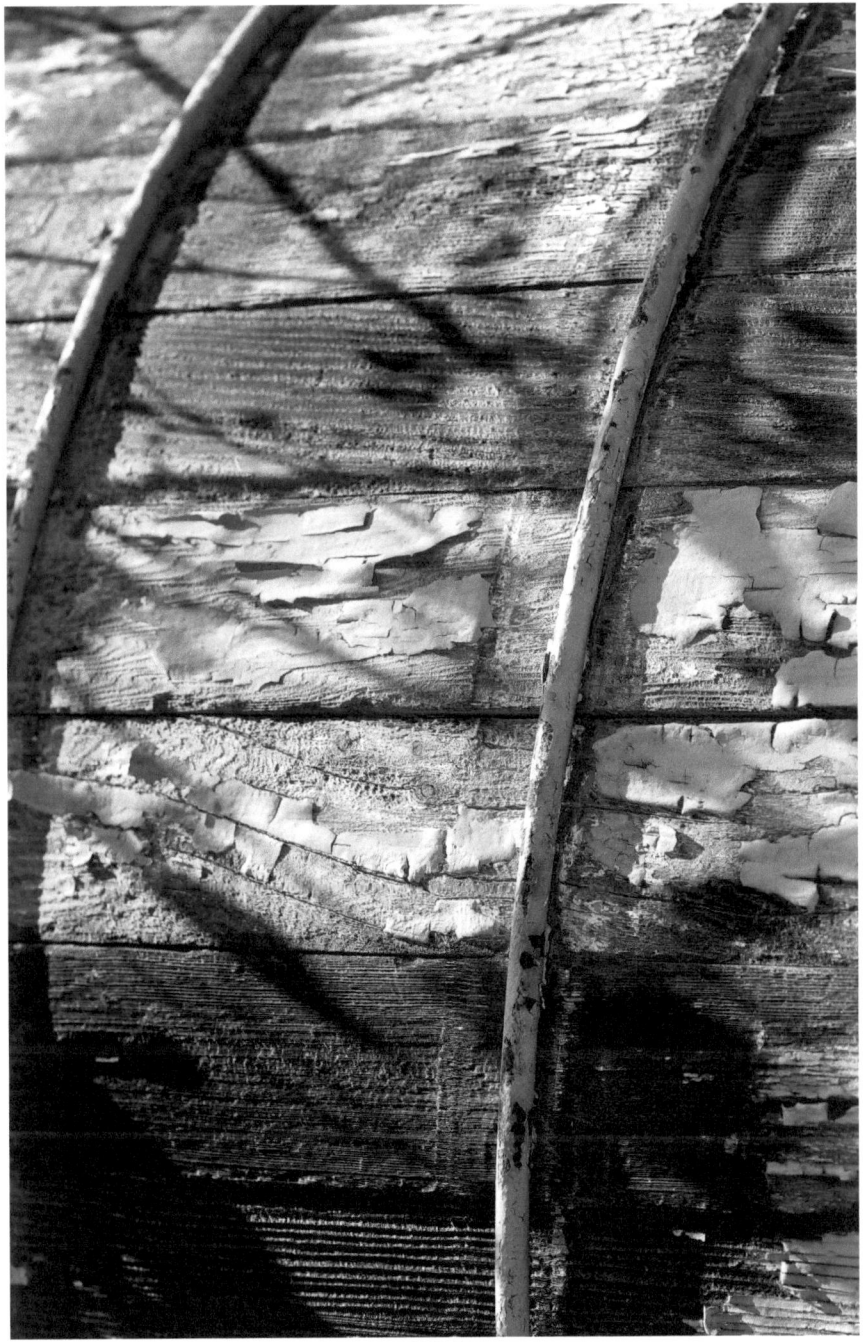

1608

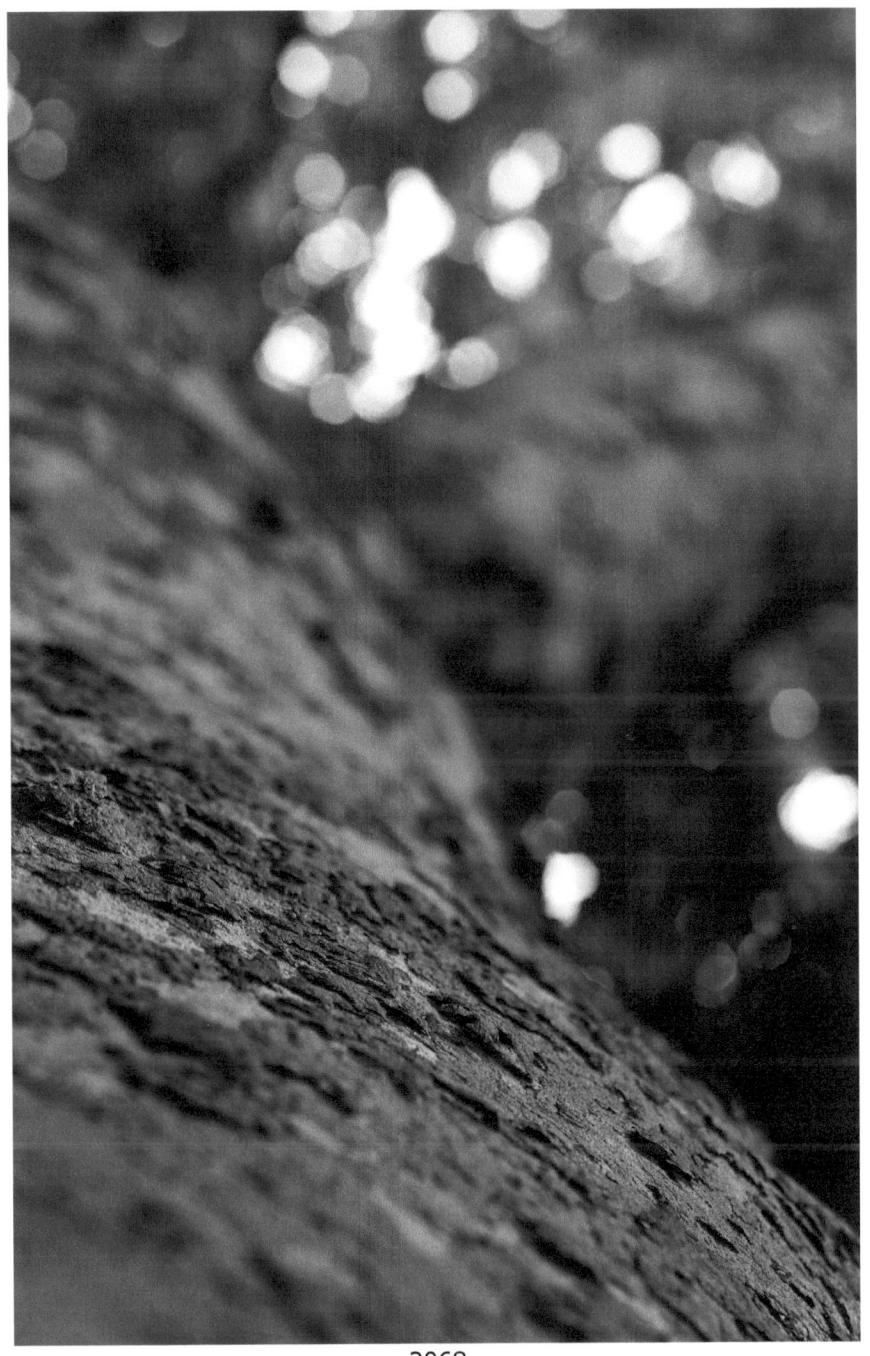

2068

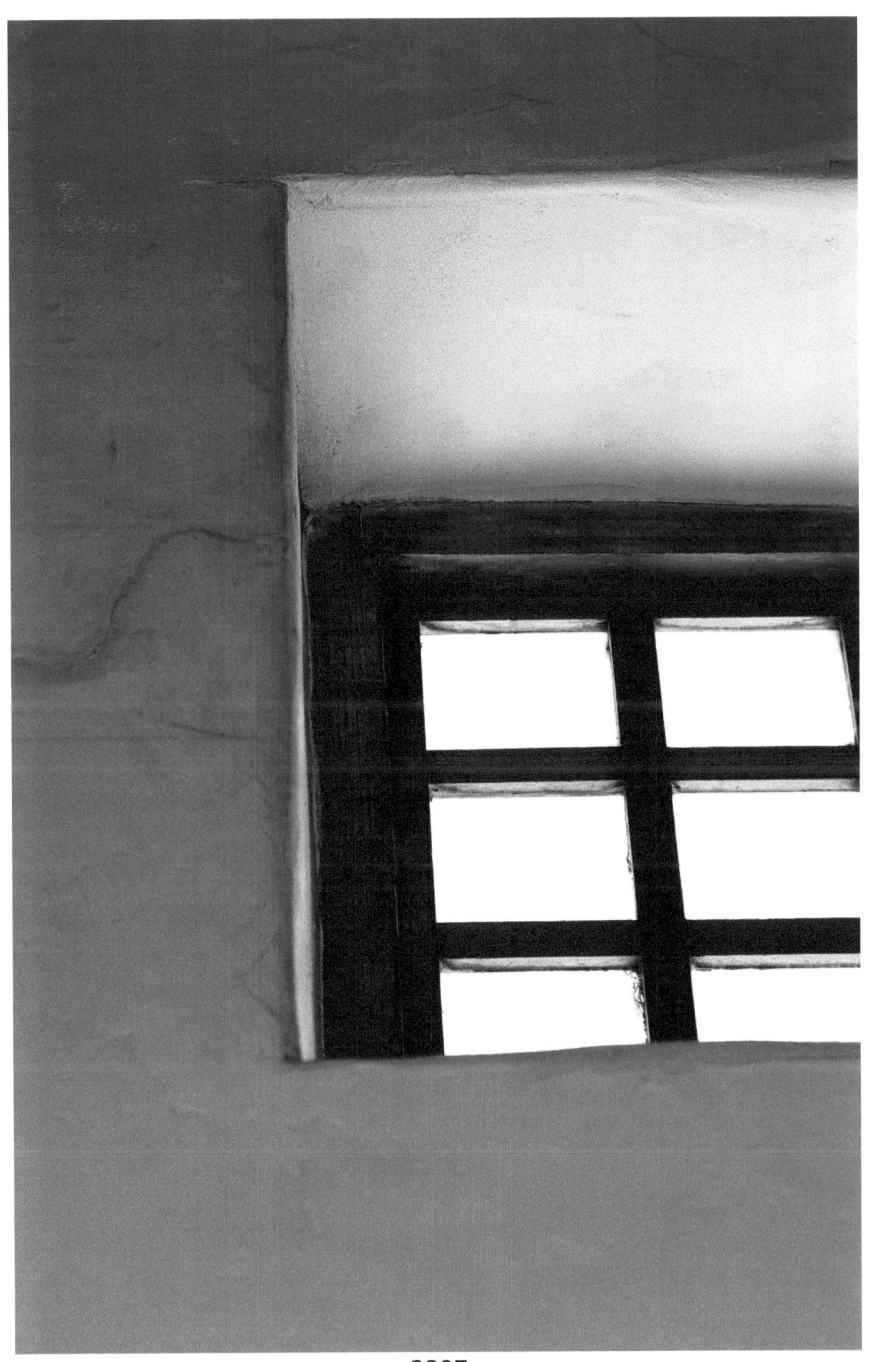

2397

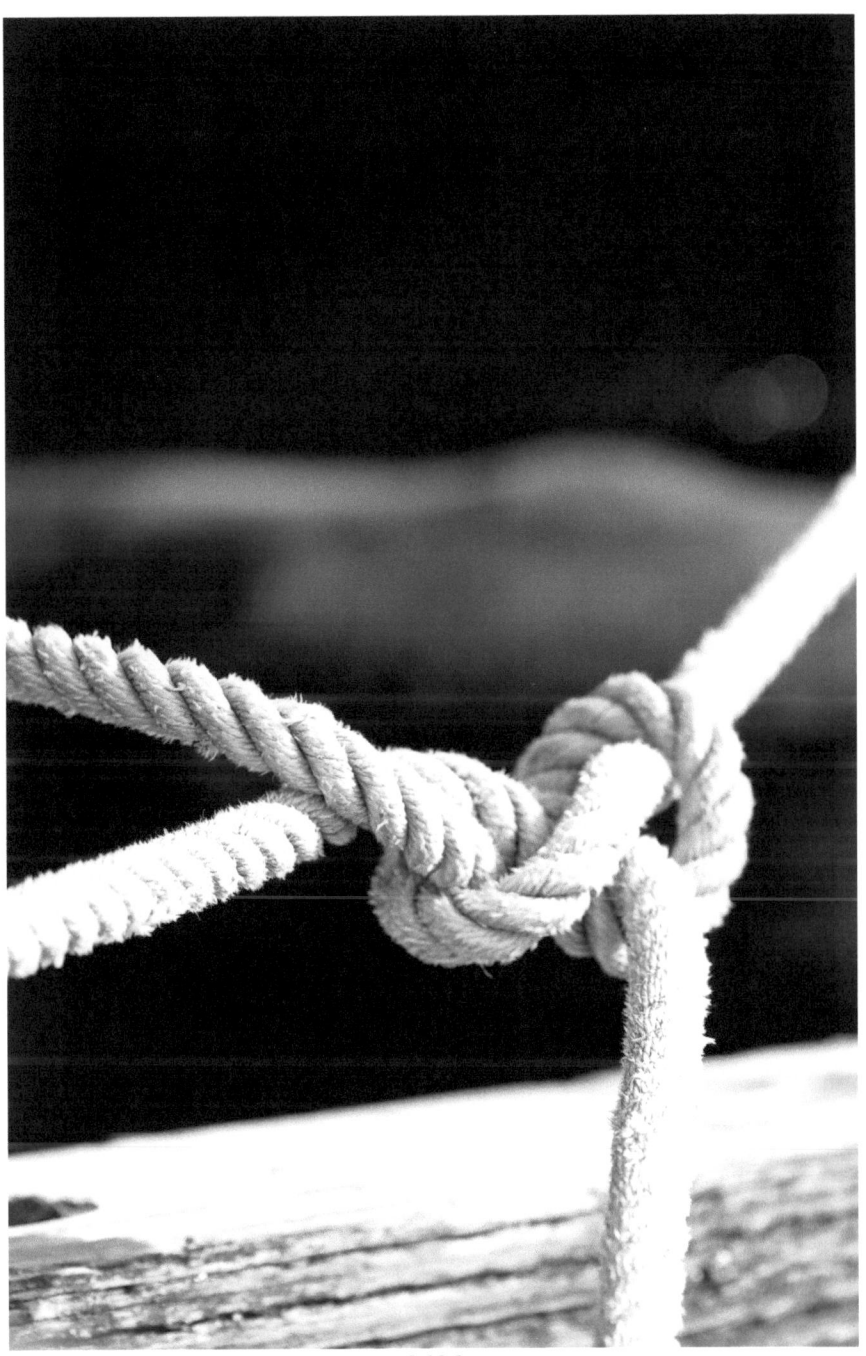

2686

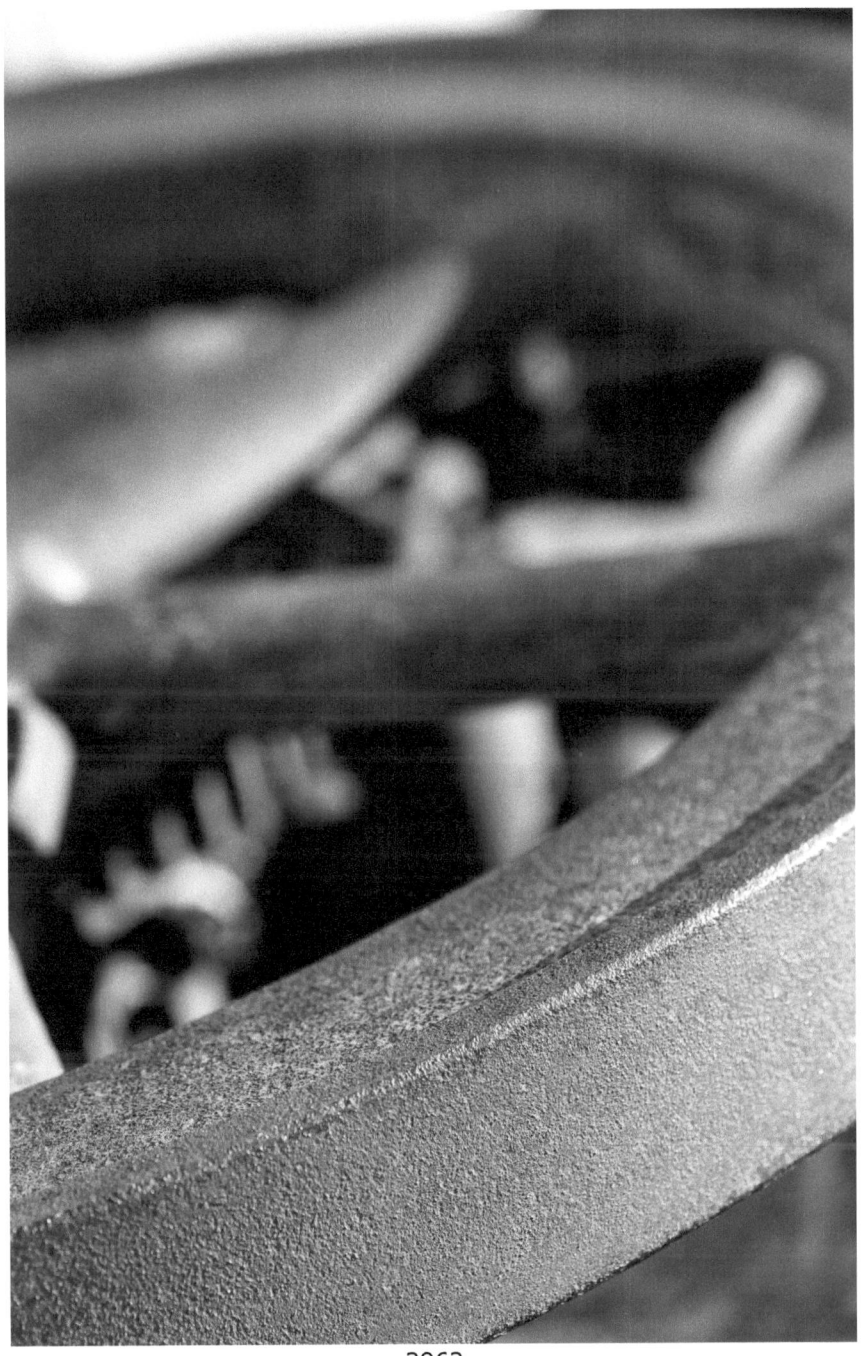

2962

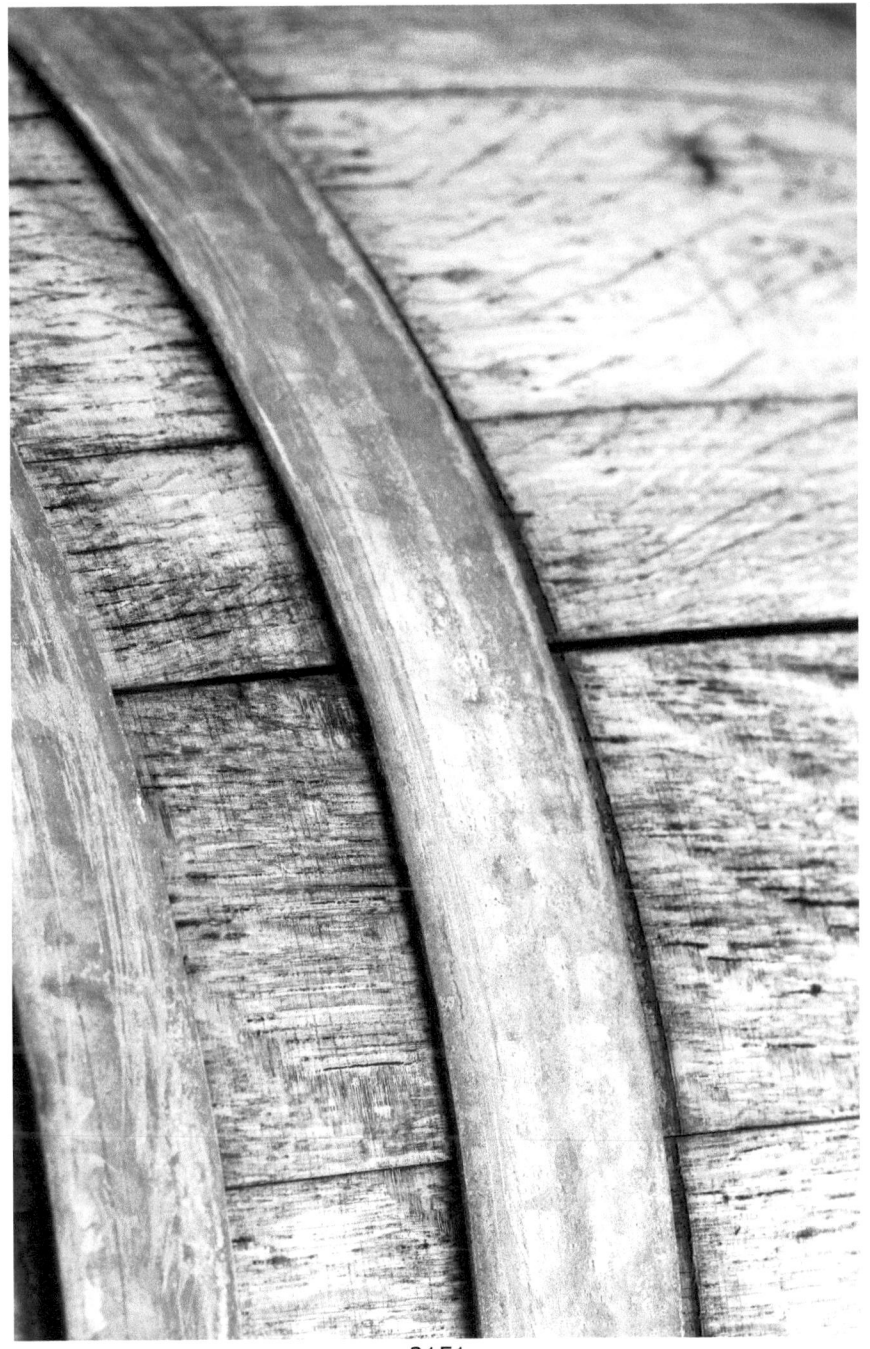

3151

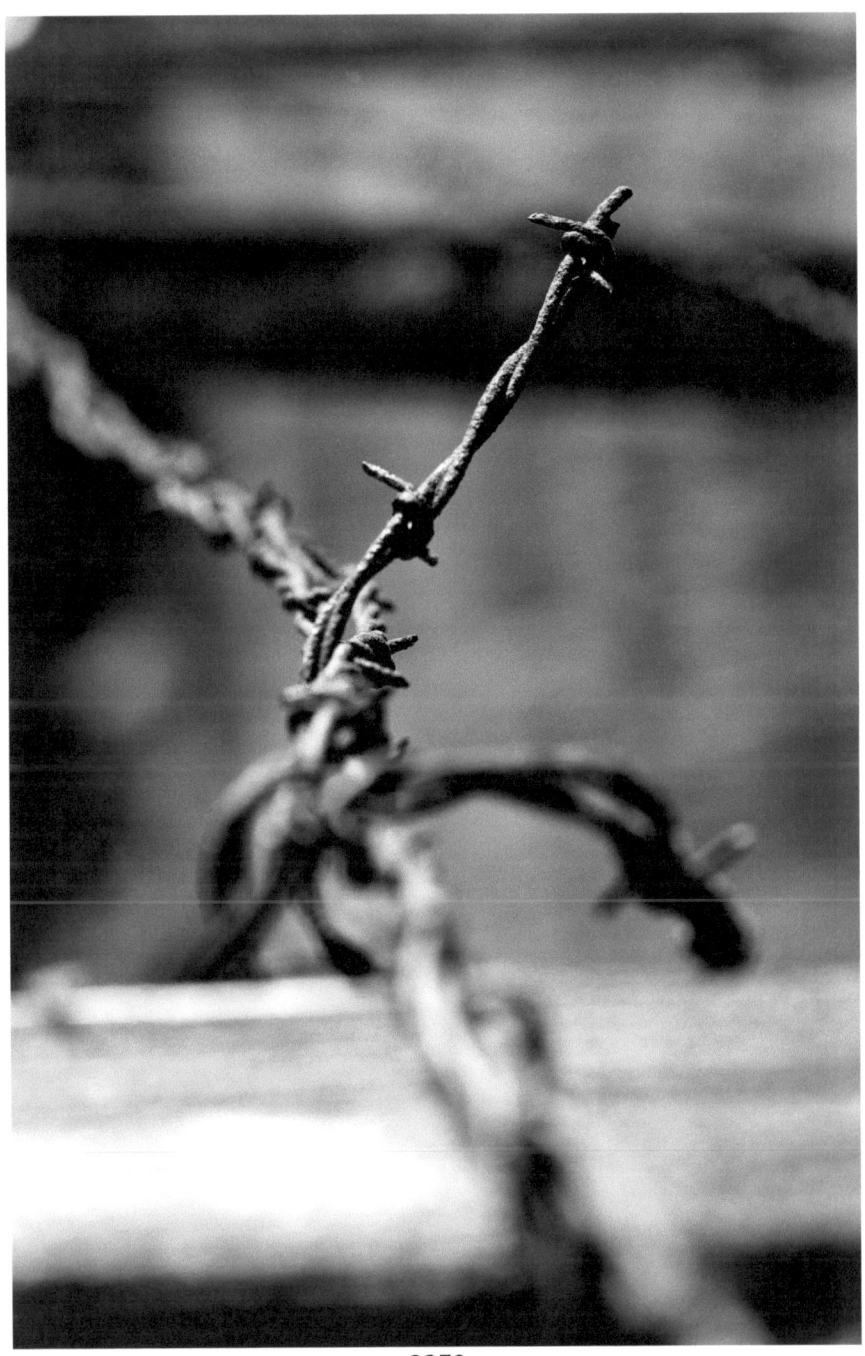

3359

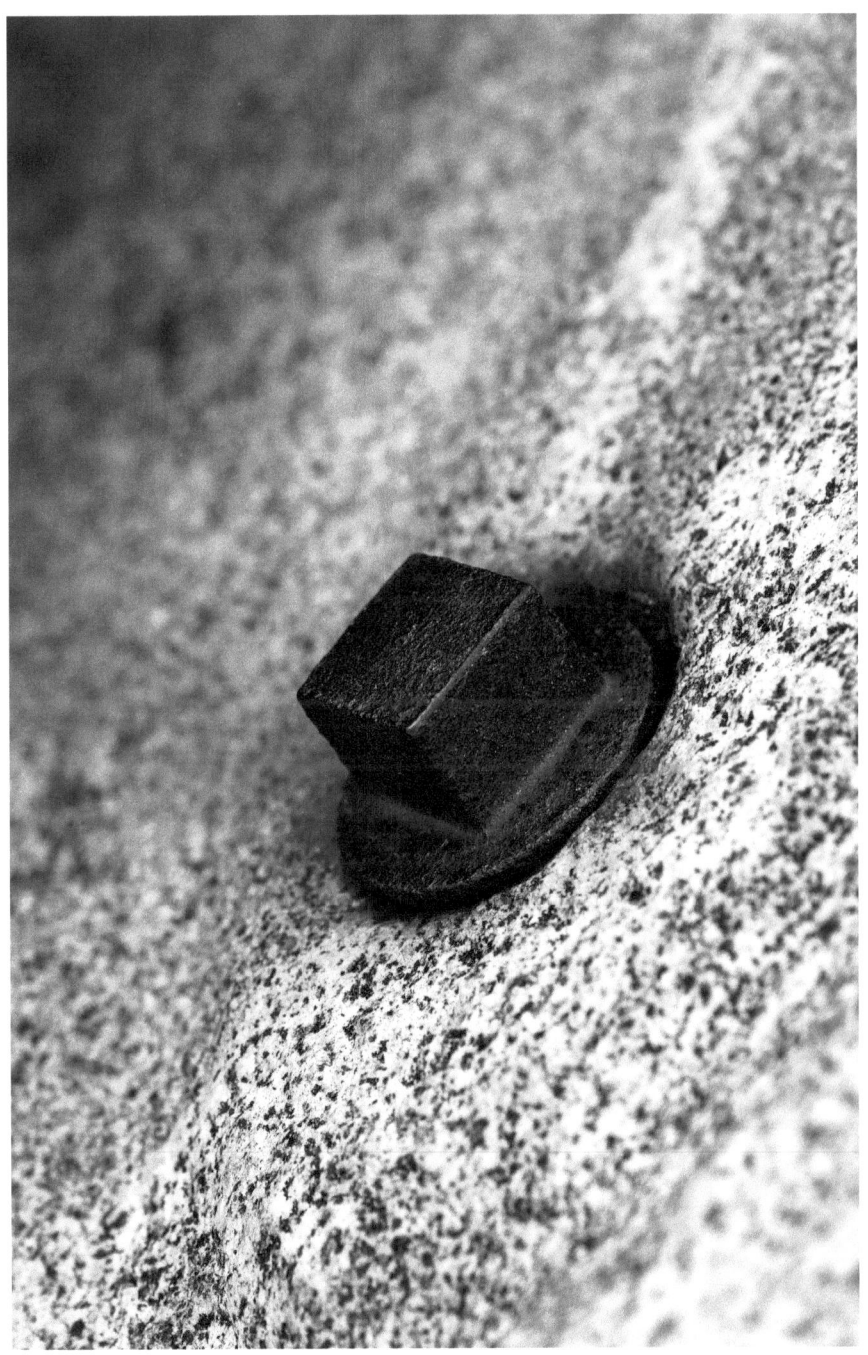

4035

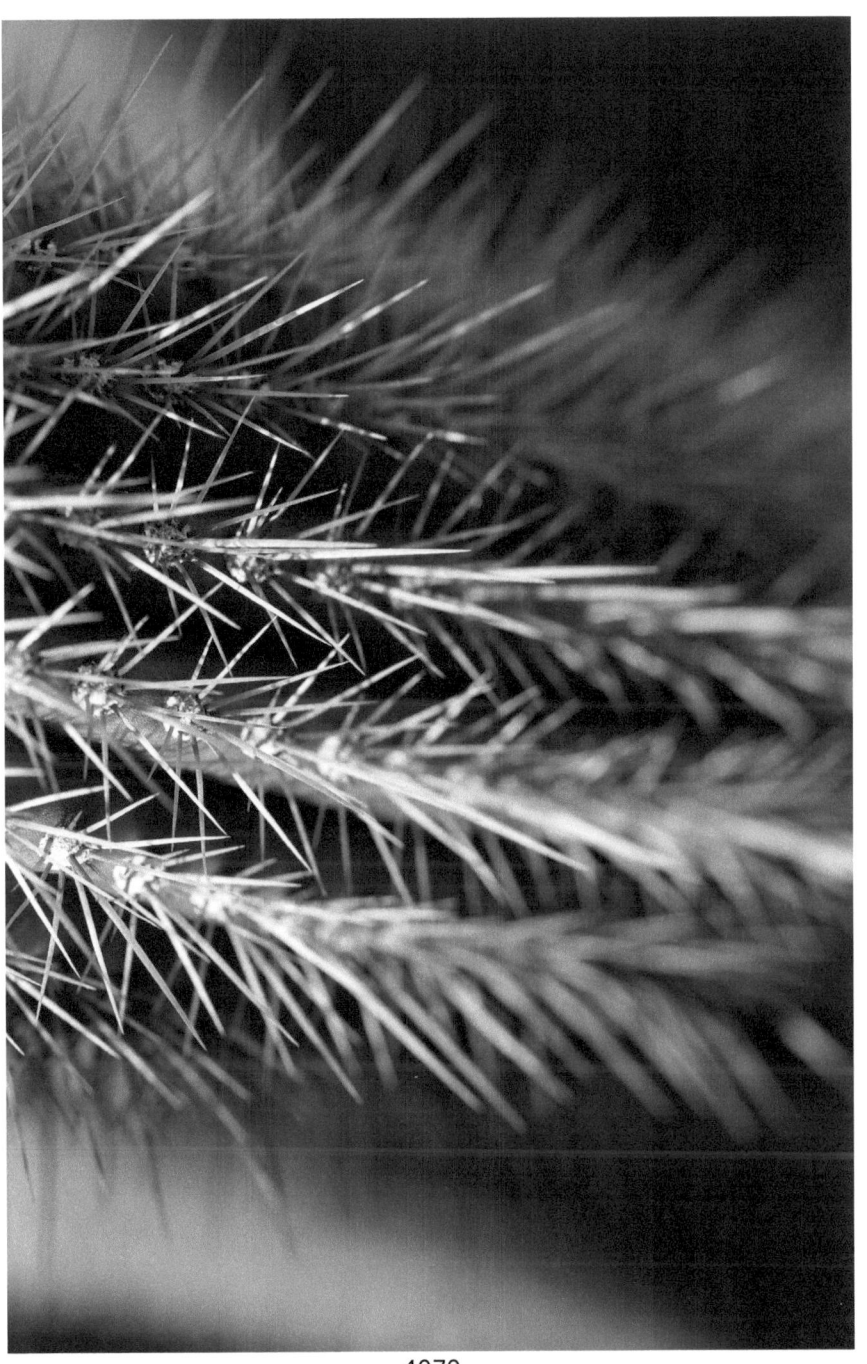

4070

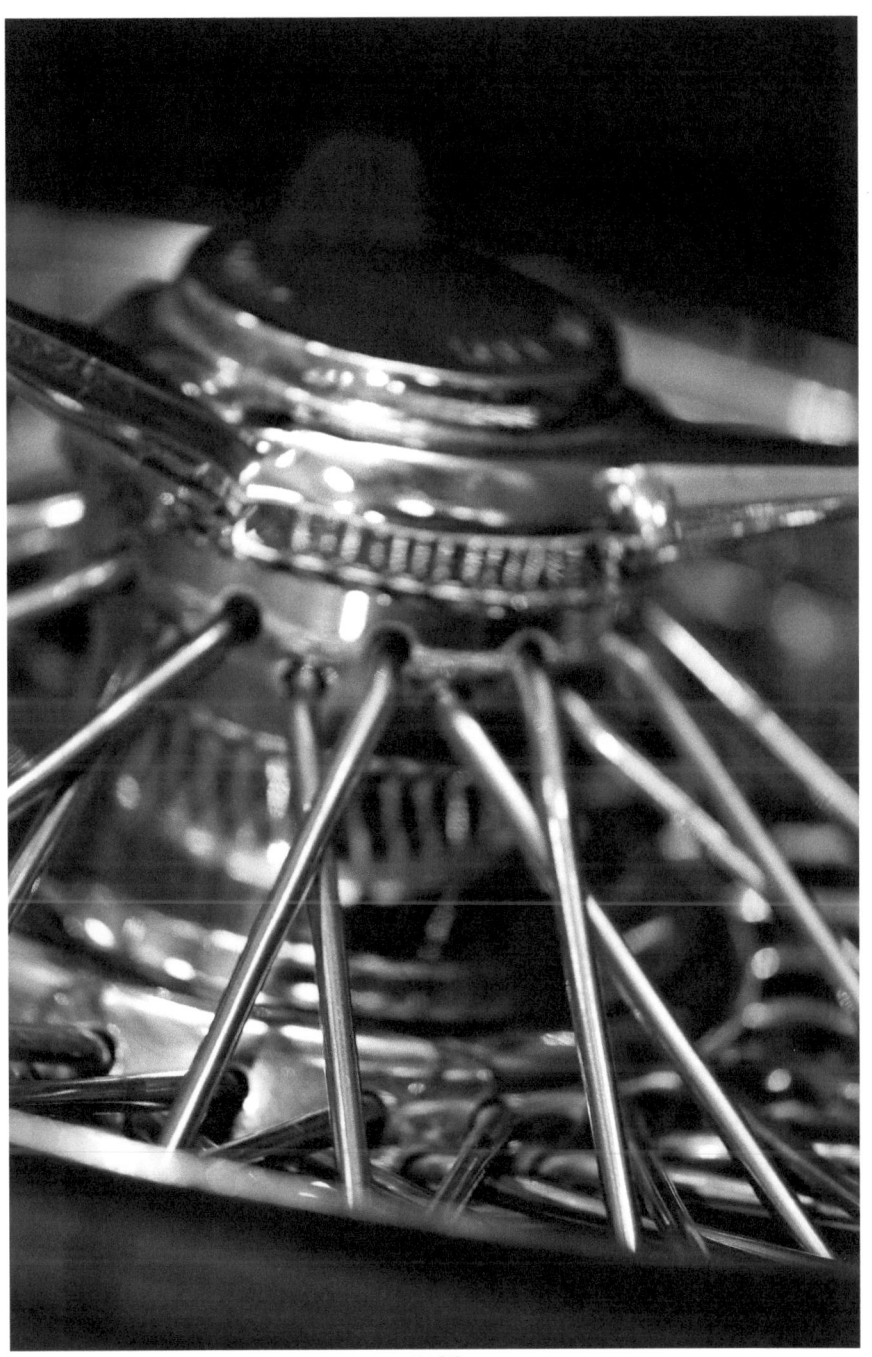

4193

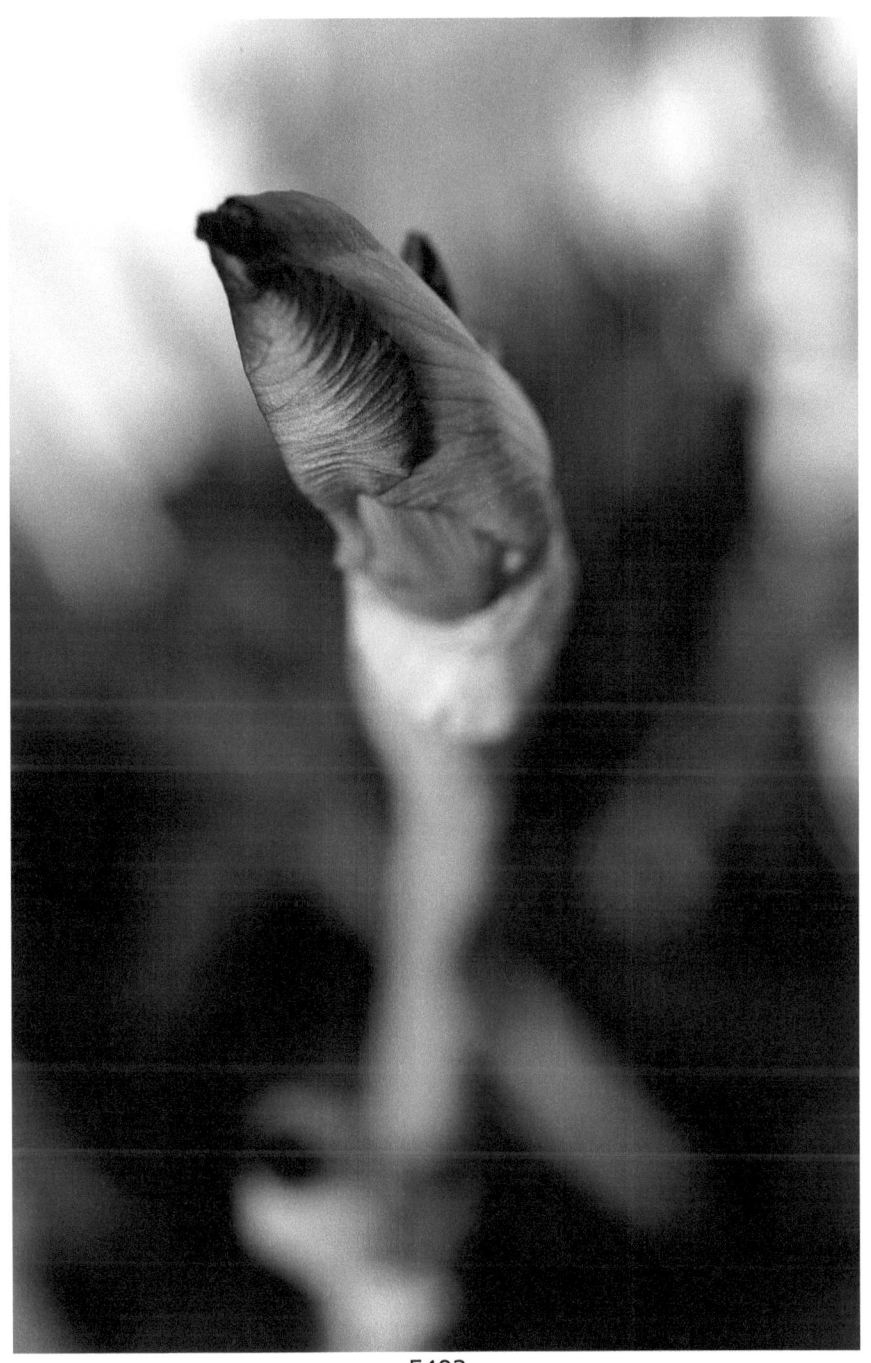

5492

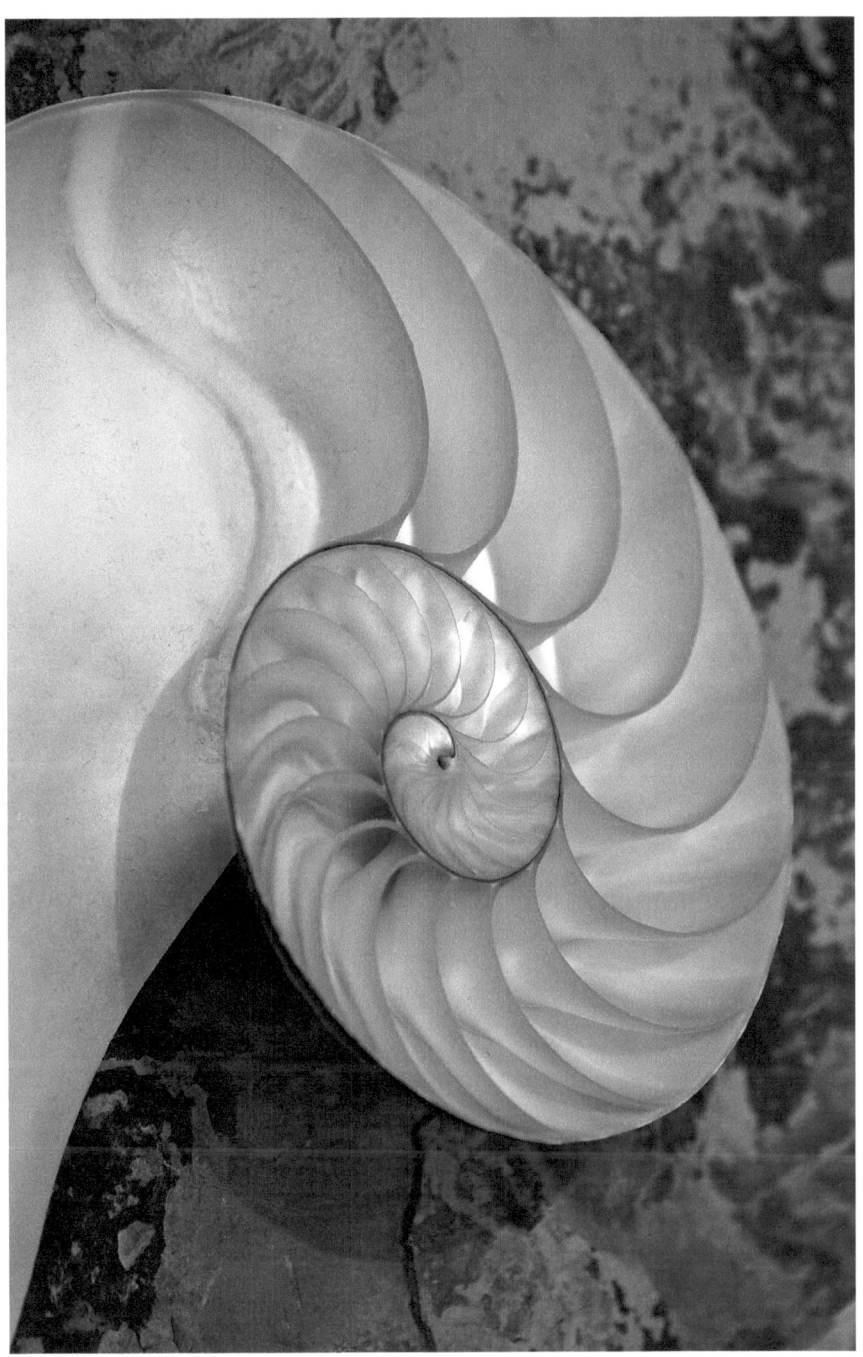

5708

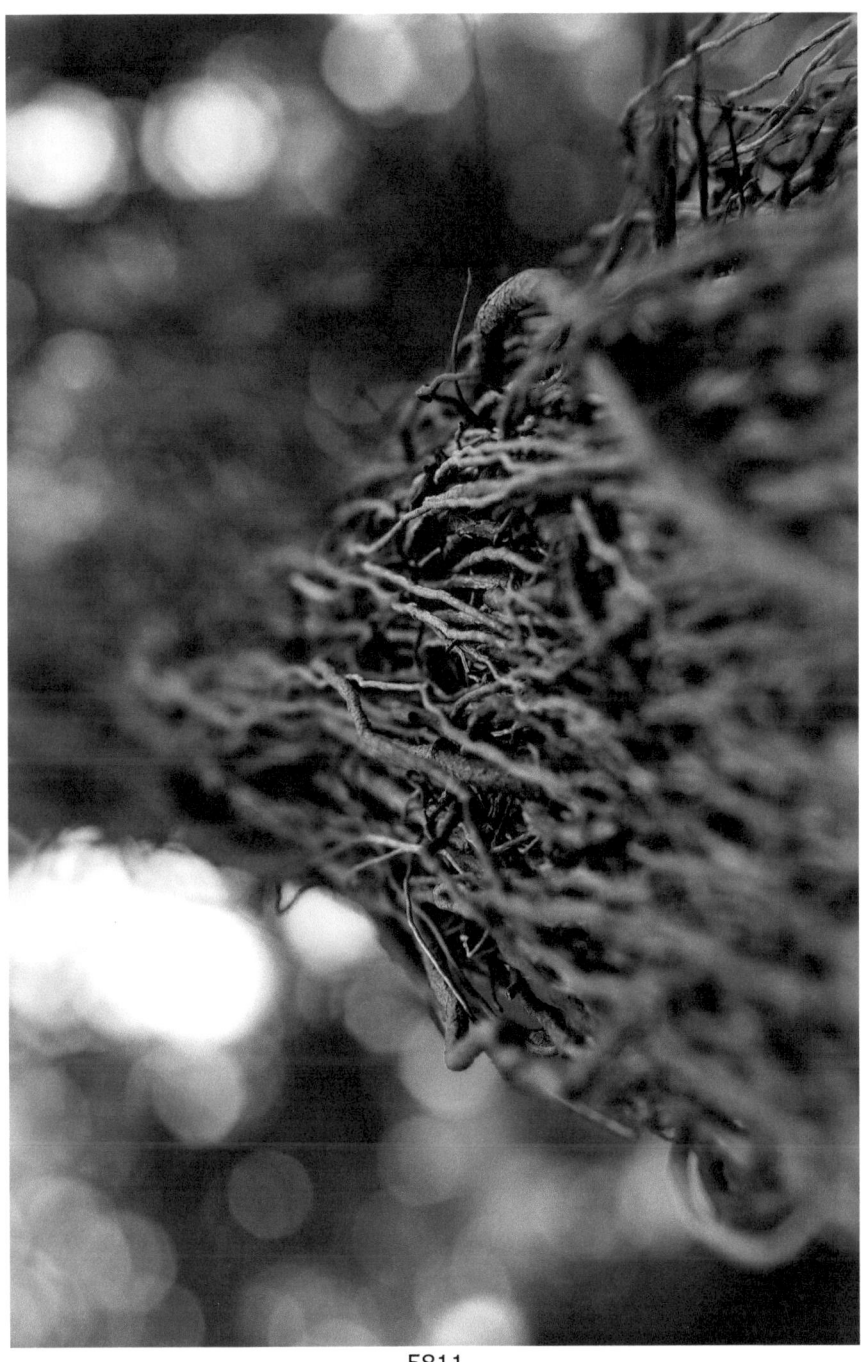

5811

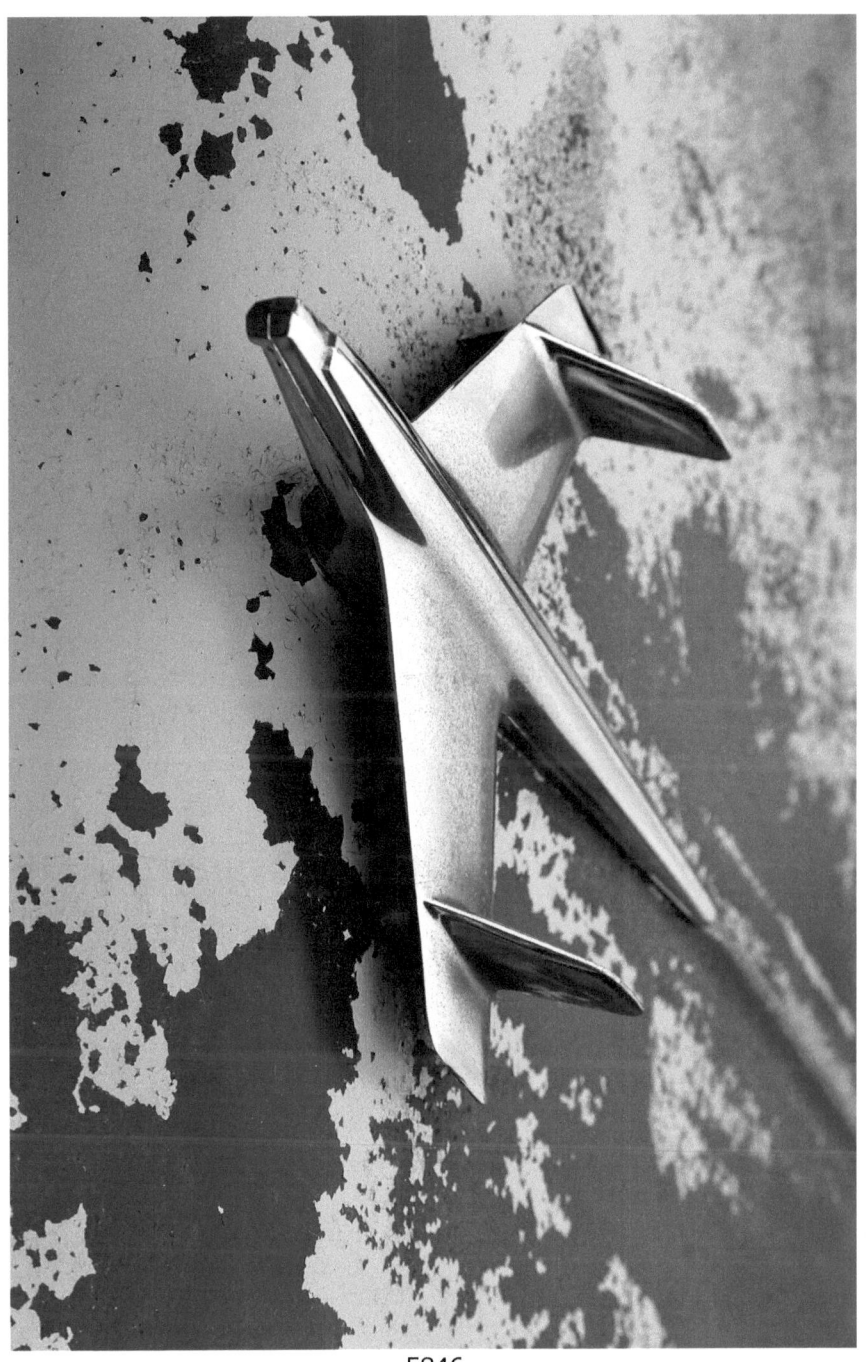

5846

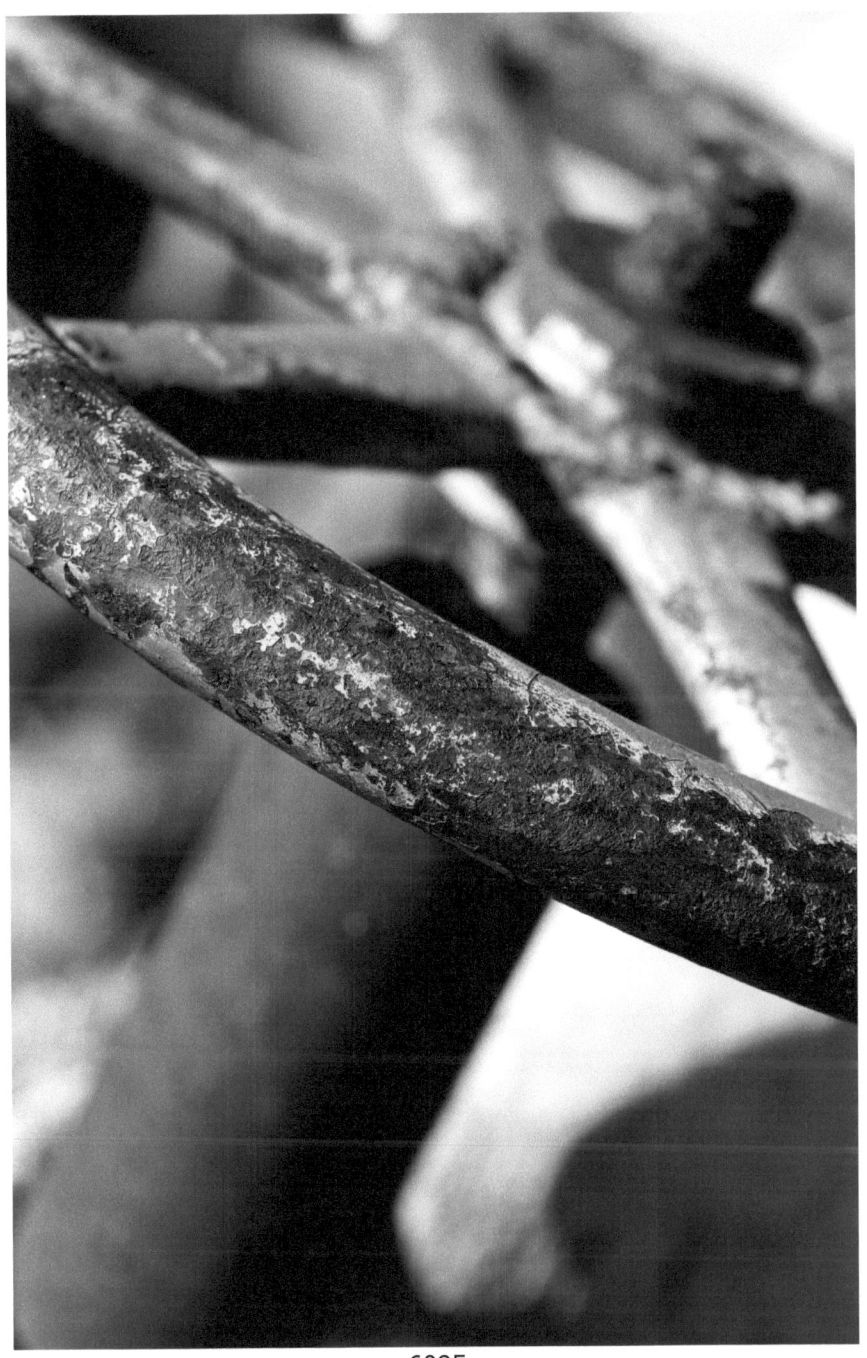

6095

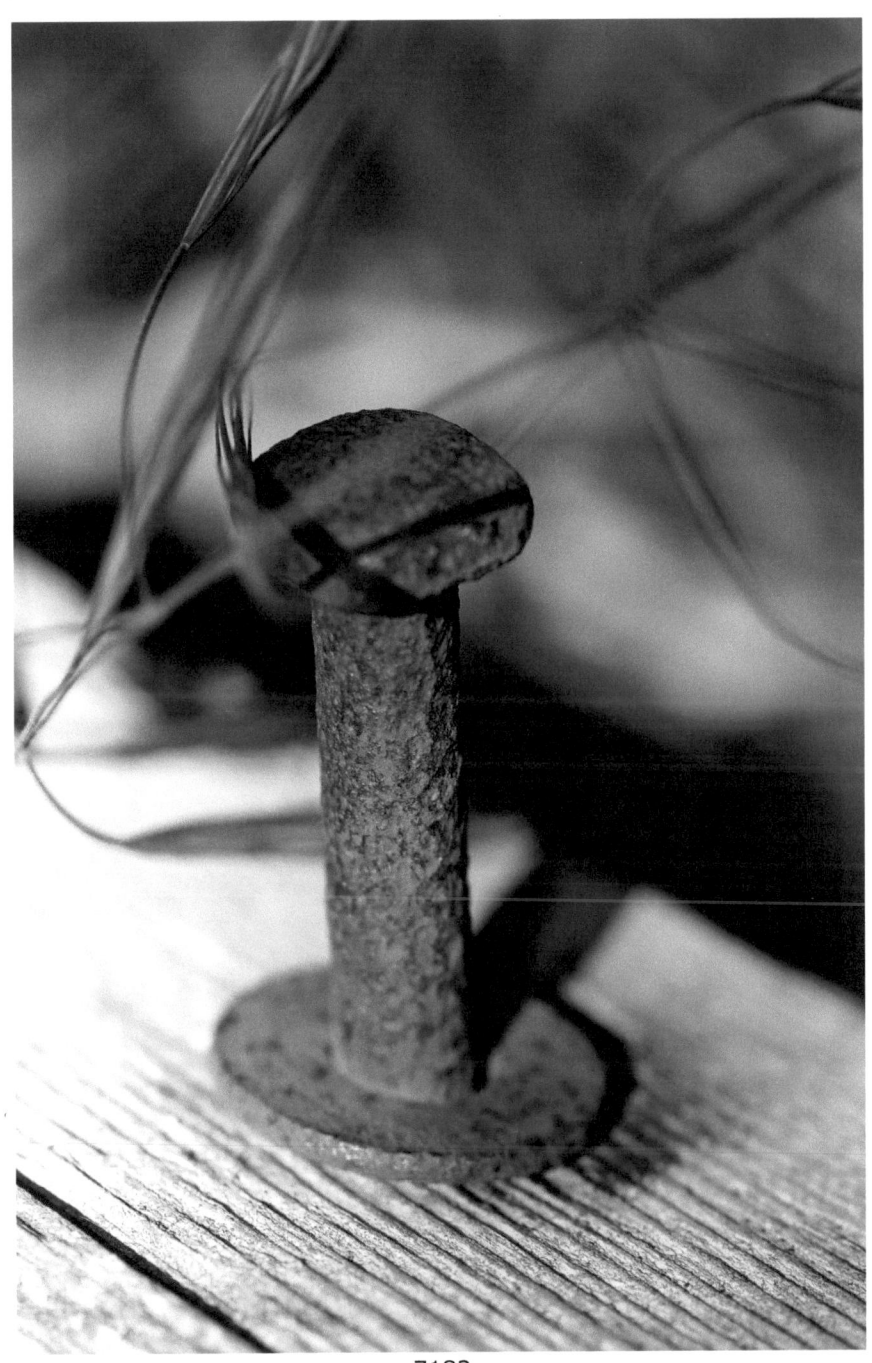

7182

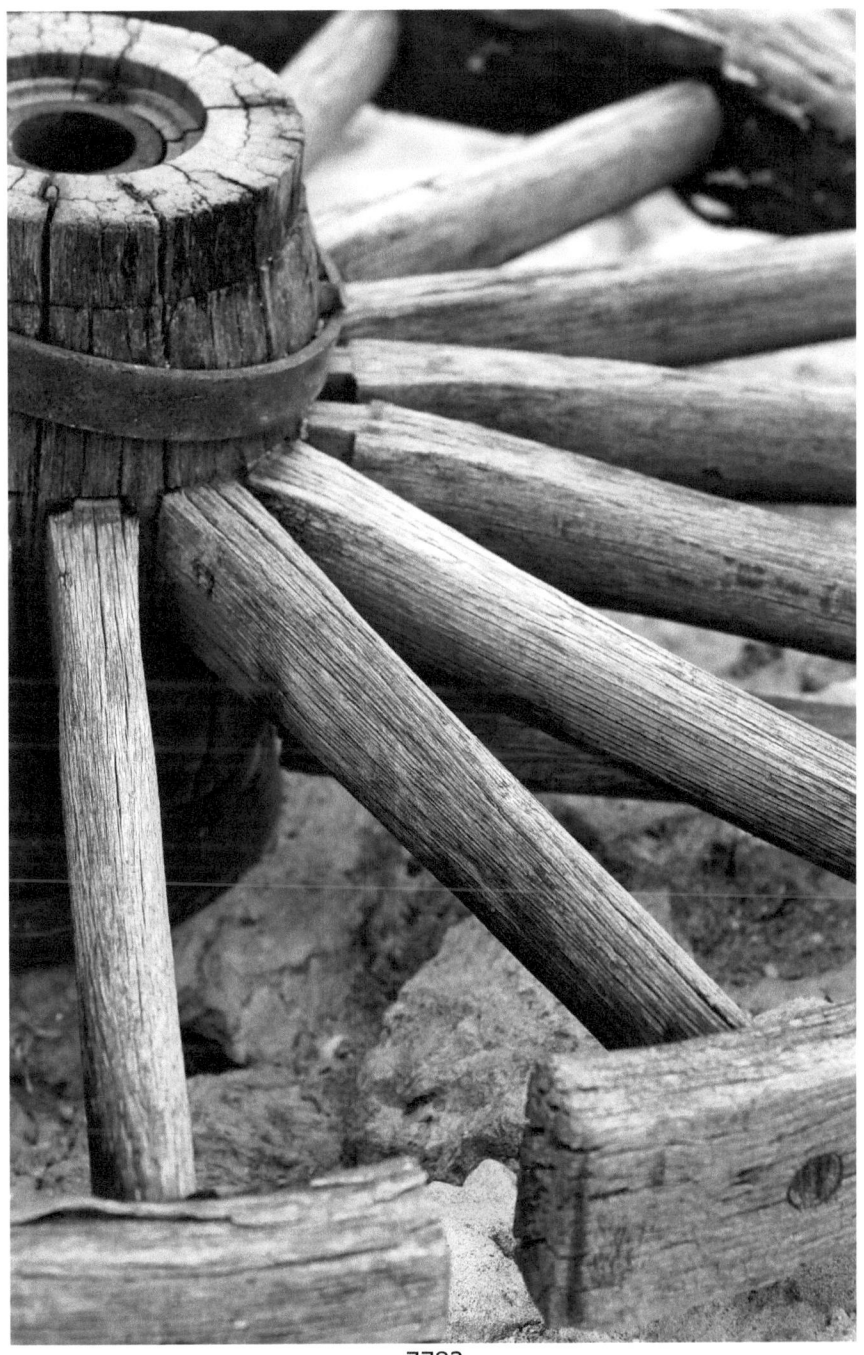

7783

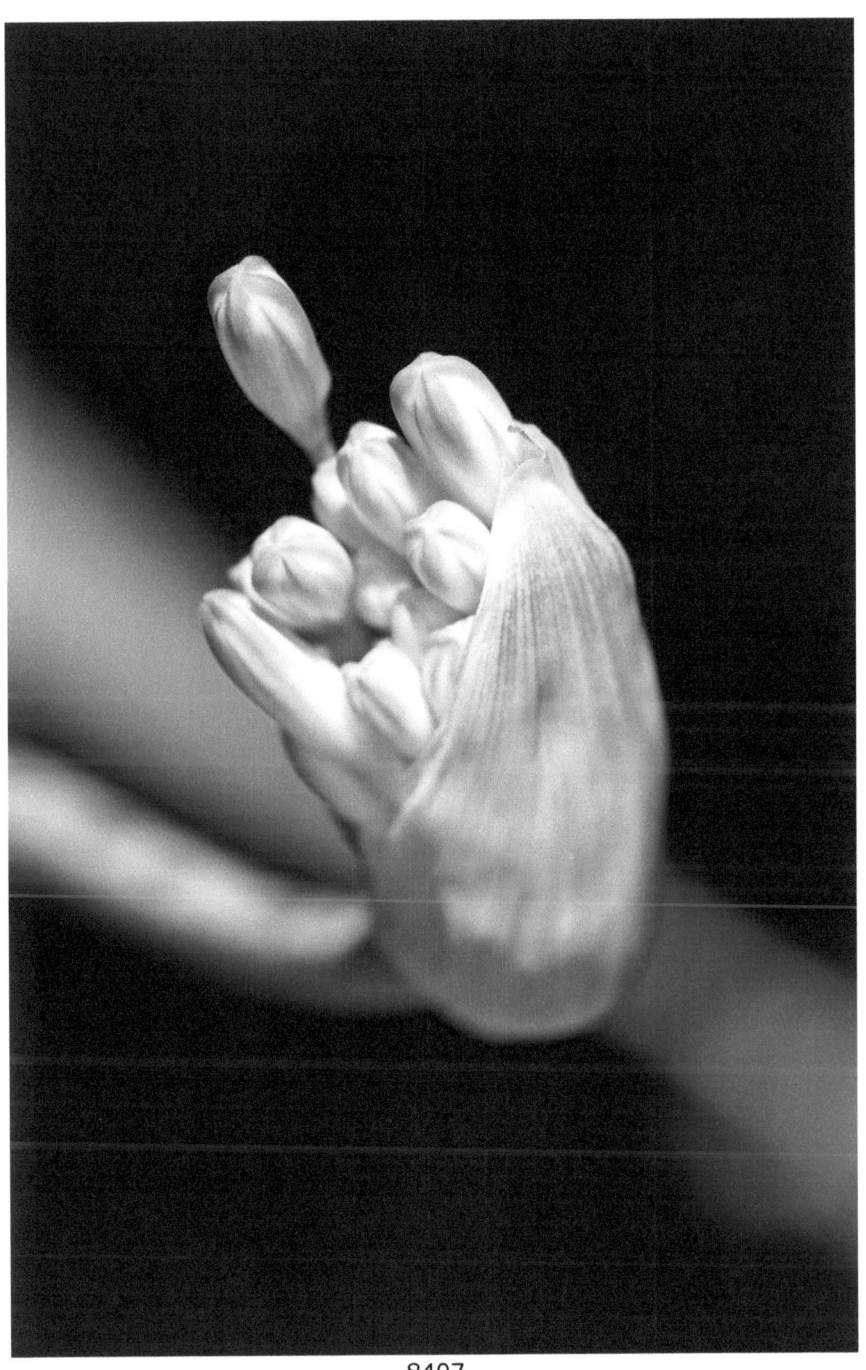

8407

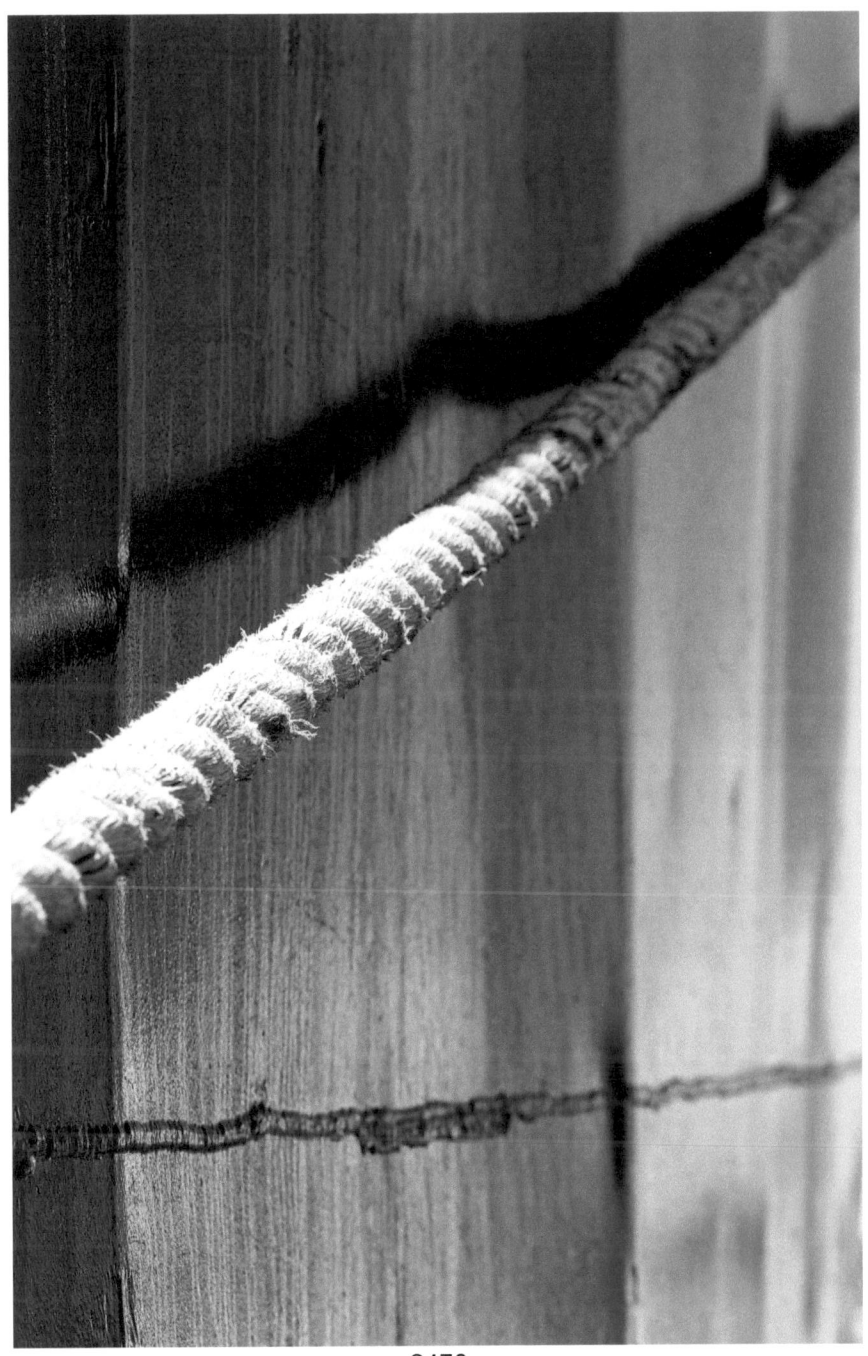

8470

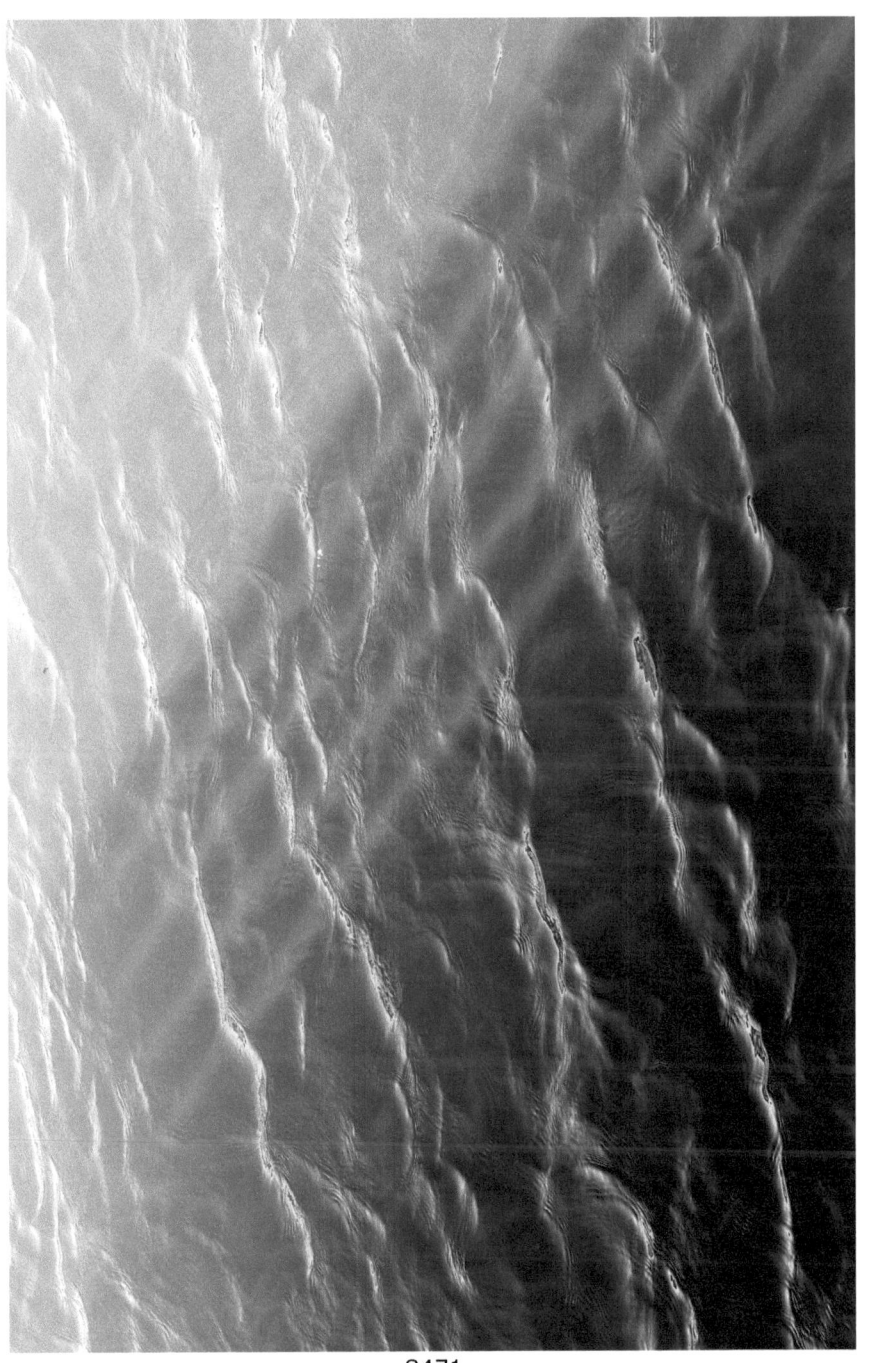

8471

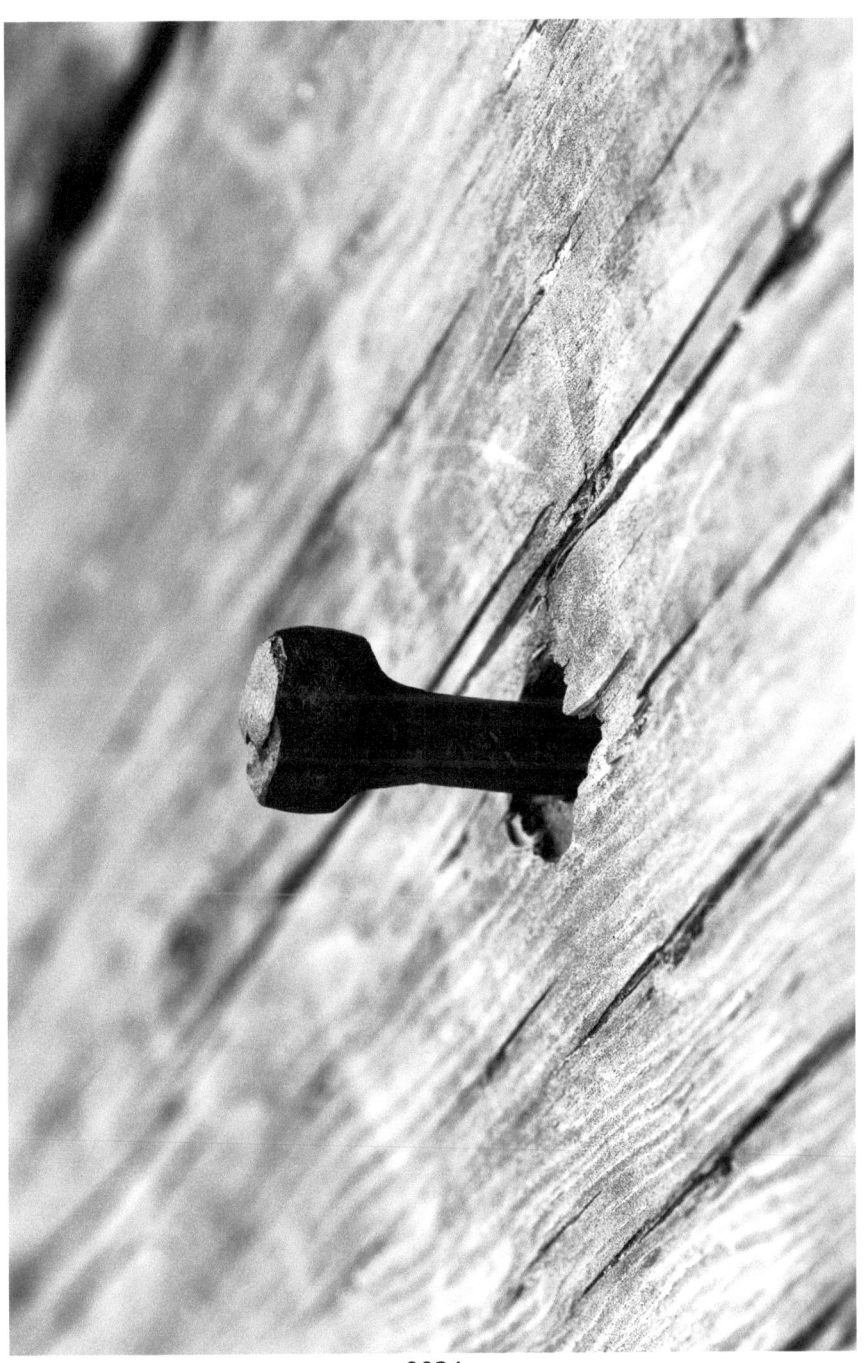

9024

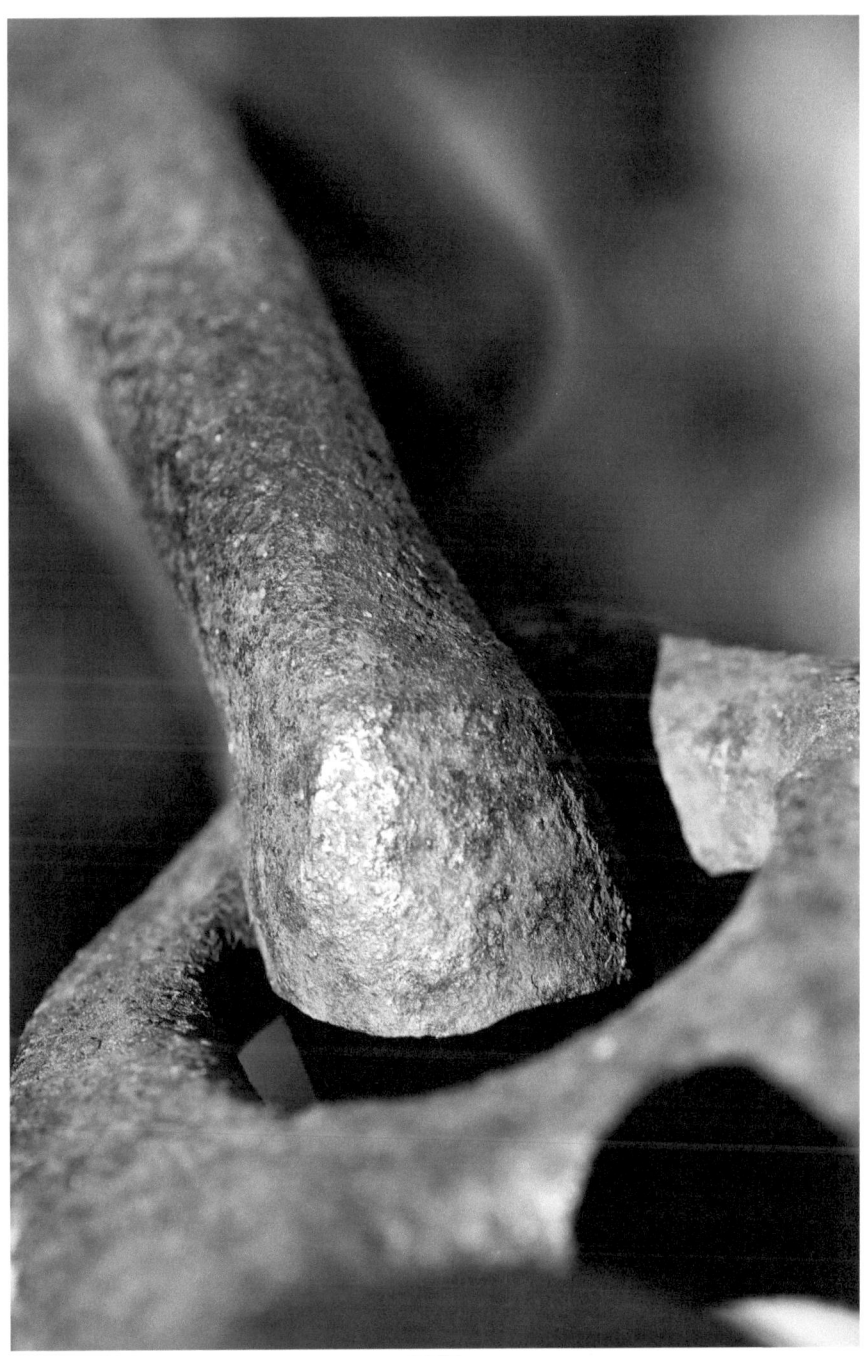

9353

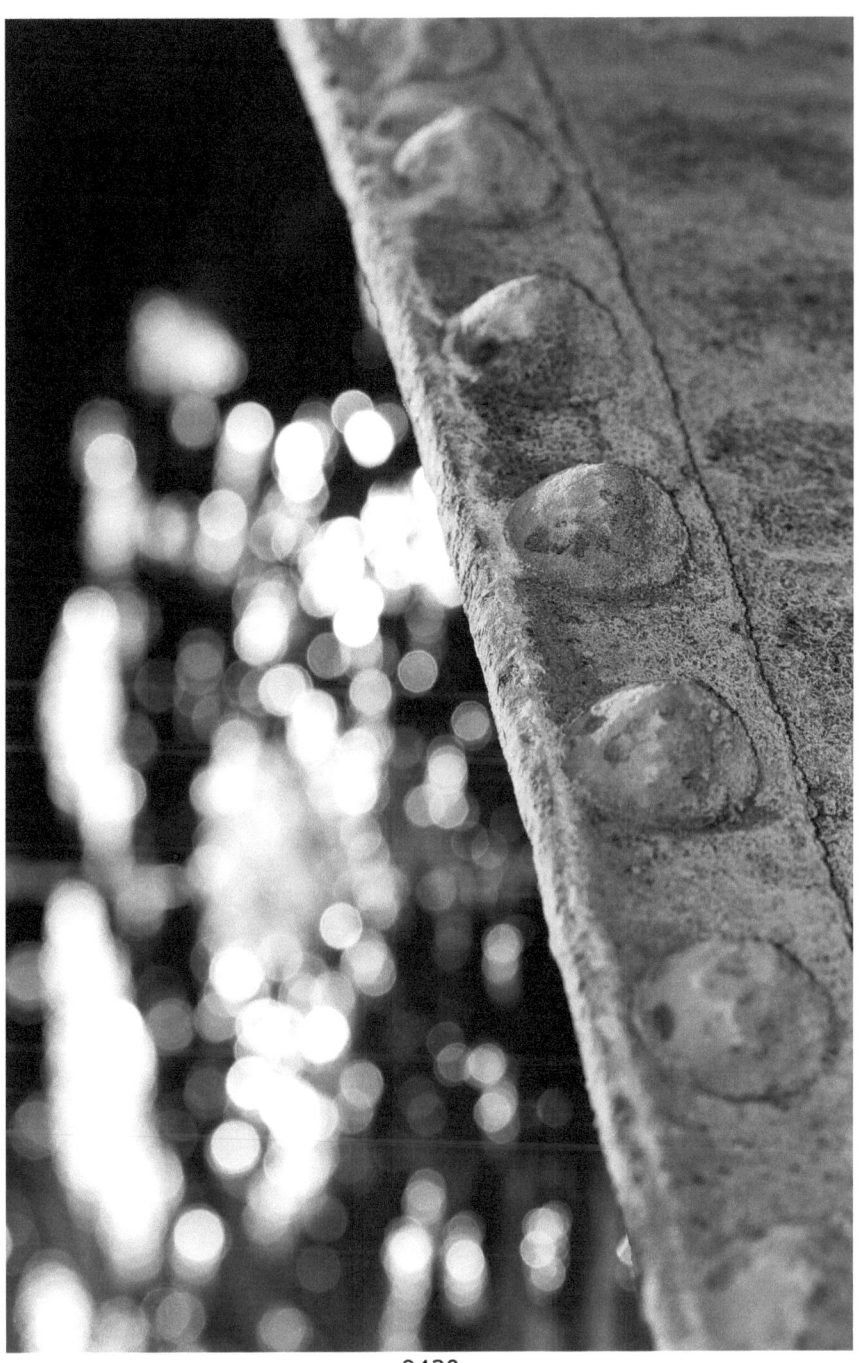

9430

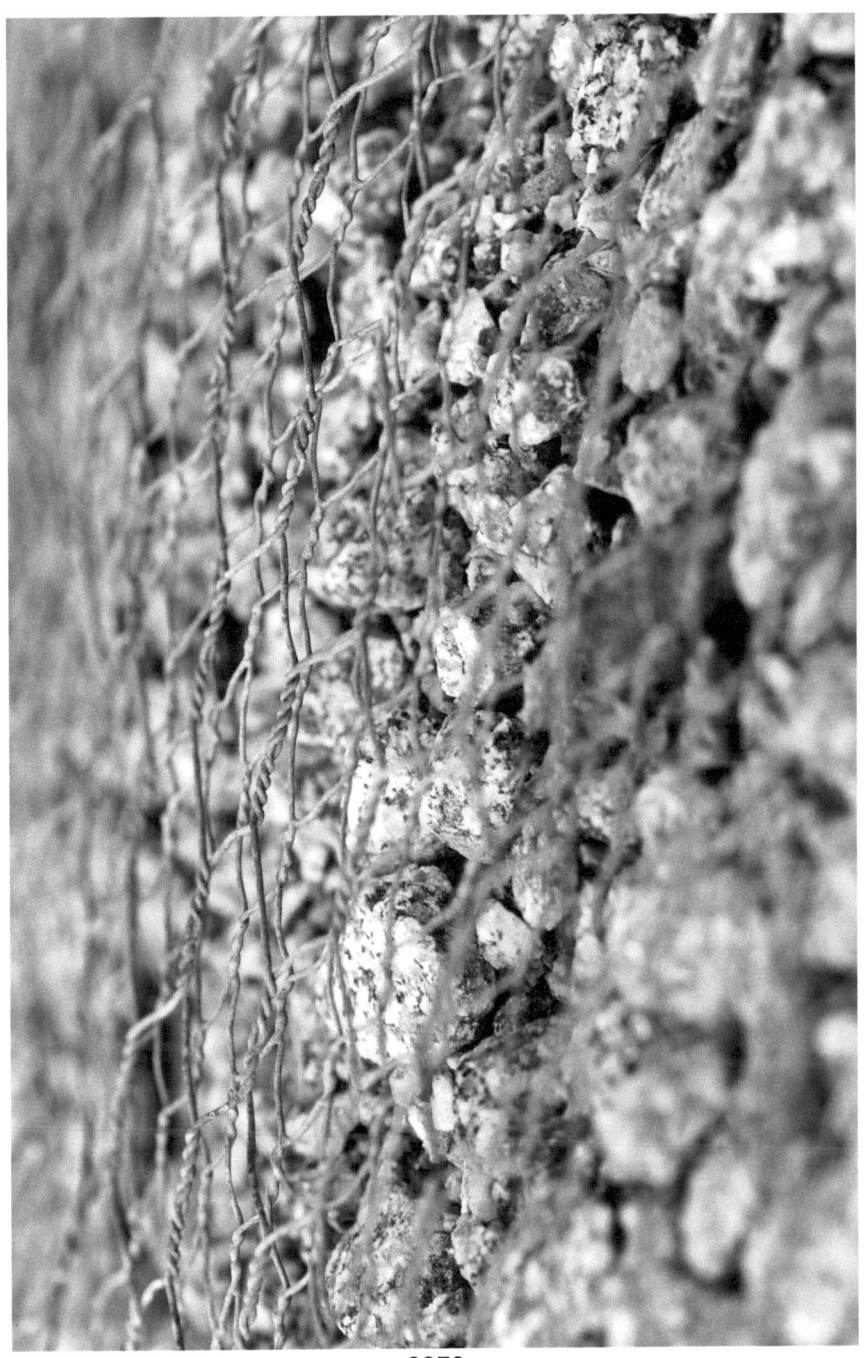

9970

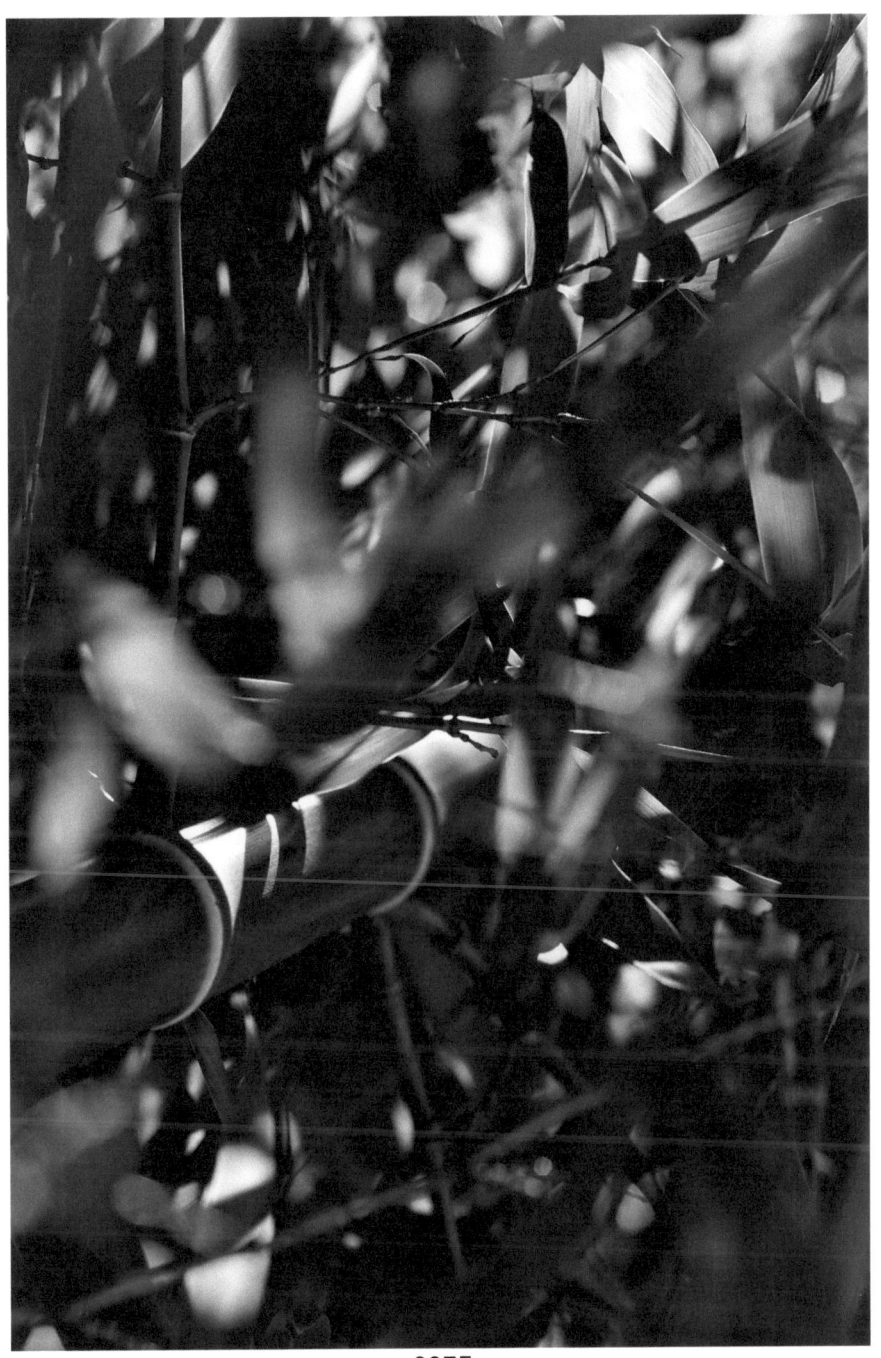

9975

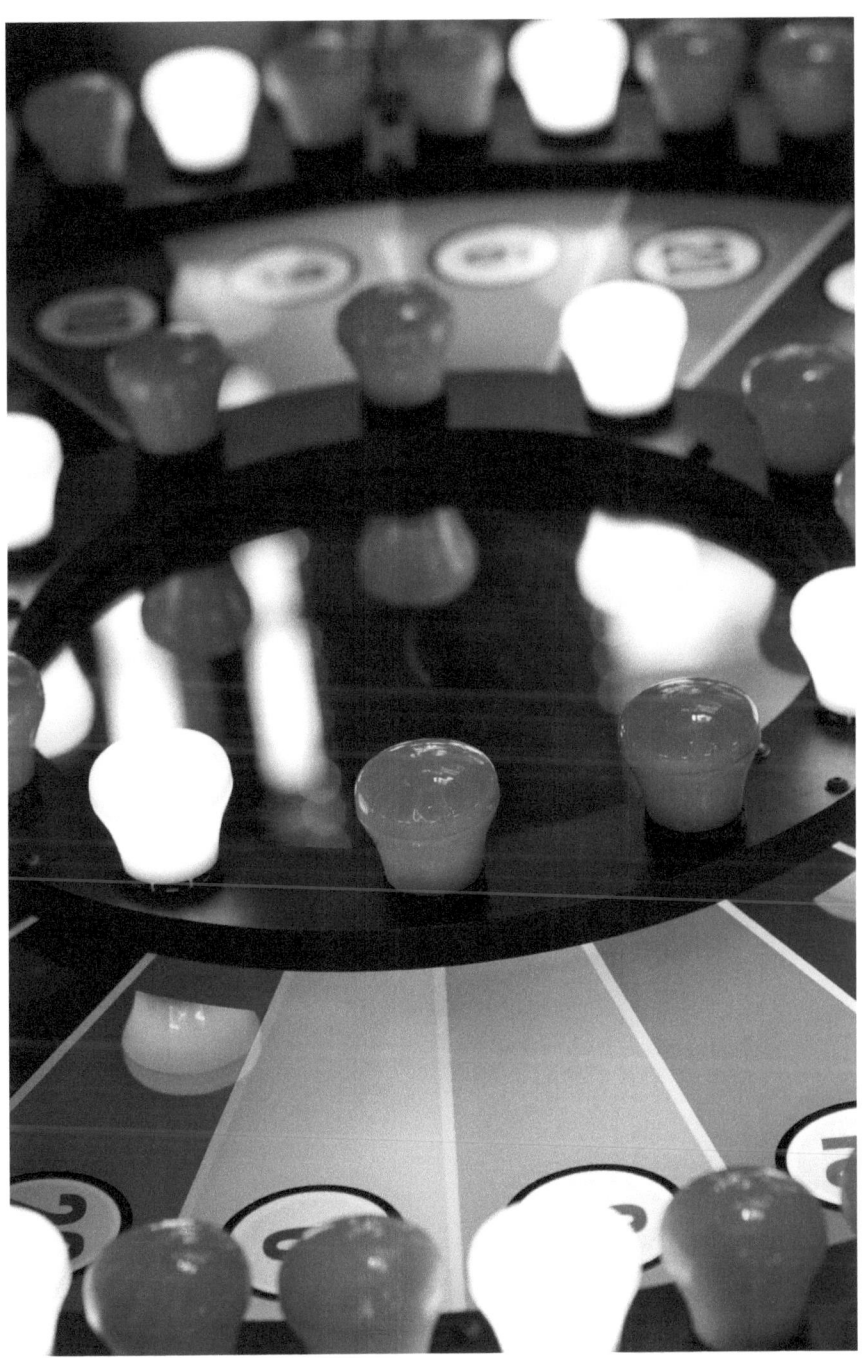

9980

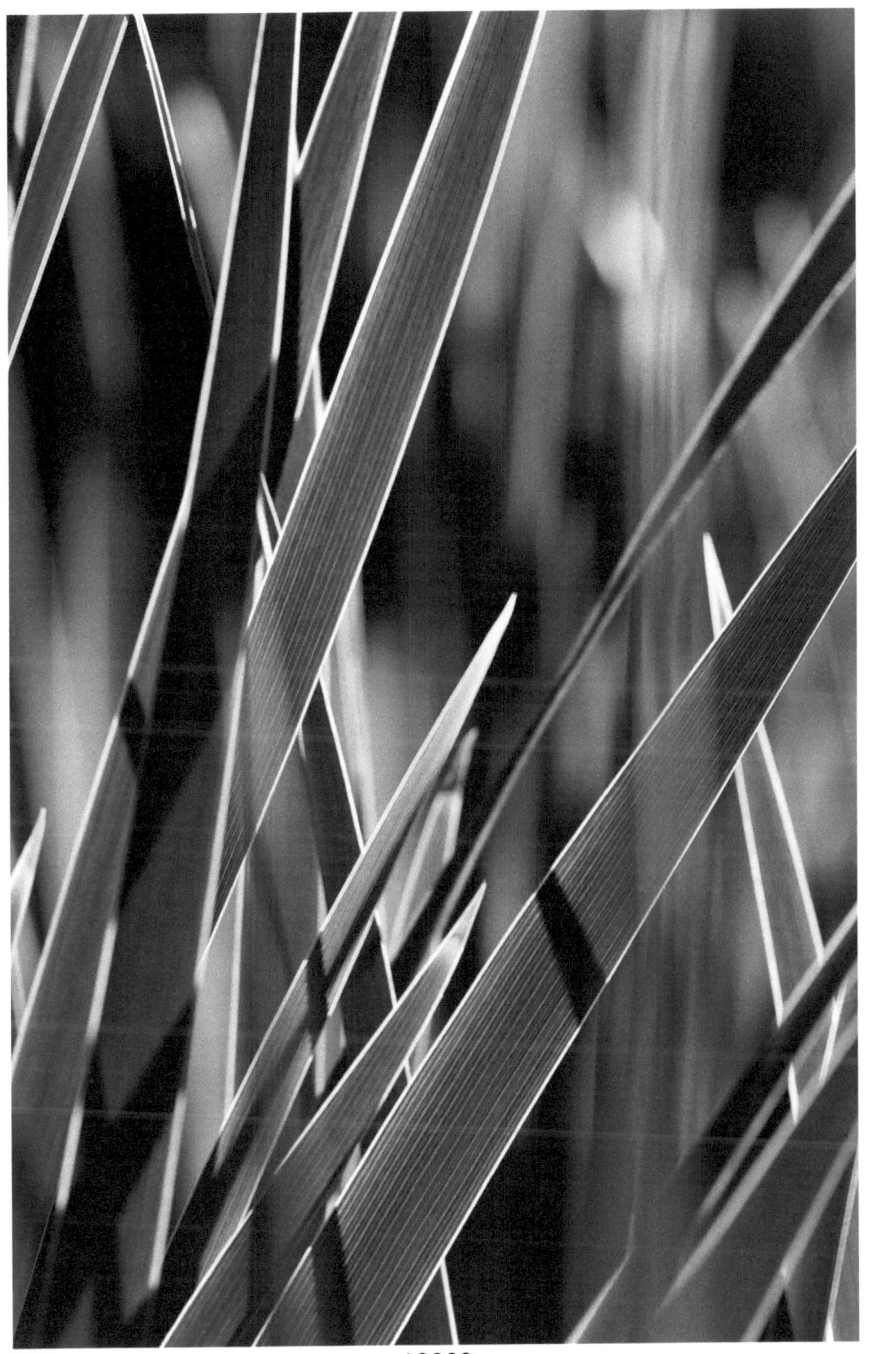

10000

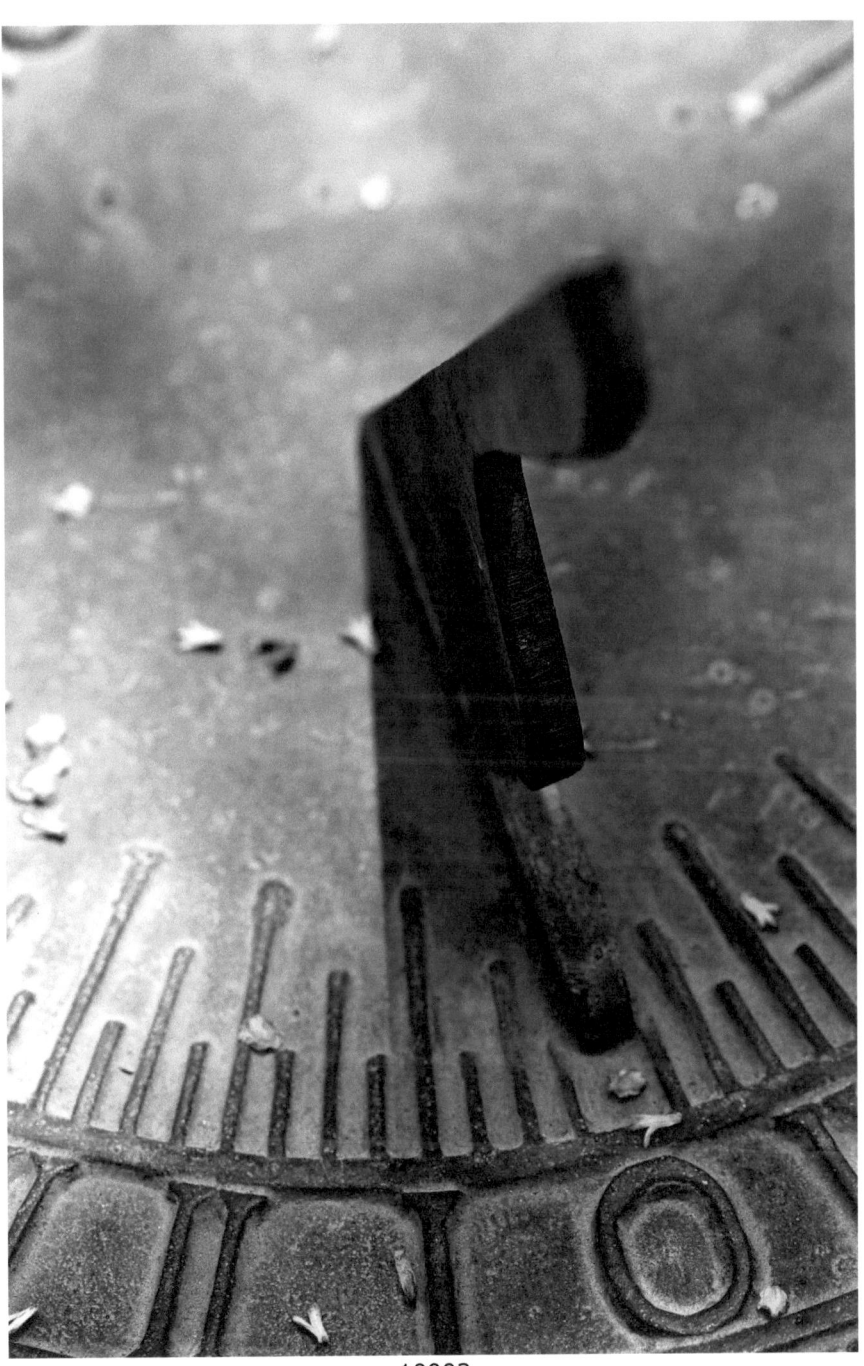

10002

www.ingramcontent.com/pod-product-compliance
Lightning Source LLC
Chambersburg PA
CBHW040836180526
45159CB00001B/204